Make, LEARN, Succeed

BUILDING A CULTURE OF CREATIVITY IN YOUR SCHOOL

Mark Gura

International Society for Technology in Education
EUGENE, OREGON • ARLINGTON, VA

Make, Learn, Succeed
Building a Culture of Creativity in Your School
Mark Gura

Editor: Emily Reed
Production Manager: Christine Longmuir
Copy Editor: Mike VanMantgem
Book Design and Production: Jeff Puda

Library of Congress Cataloging-in-Publication Data available.

First Edition
ISBN: 978-1-56484-380-7
Ebook version available.

Printed in the United States of America

About ISTE

The International Society for Technology in Education (ISTE) is the premier non-profit organization serving educators and education leaders committed to empowering connected learners in a connected world. ISTE serves more than 100,000 education stakeholders throughout the world. ISTE's innovative offerings include the ISTE Conference & Expo, one of the biggest, most comprehensive ed tech events in the world—as well as the widely adopted ISTE Standards for learning, teaching and leading in the digital age and a robust suite of professional learning resources, including webinars, online courses, consulting services for schools and districts, books, and peer-reviewed journals and publications. Visit iste.org to learn more.

Also by Mark Gura

Teaching Literacy in the Digital Age: Inspiration for All Levels and Literacies (Editor)

Getting Started with LEGO Robotics: A Guide for K-12 Educators

Related ISTE Titles

Innovation Age Learning: Empowering Students by Empowering Teachers, by Sam Sakai-Miller

To see all books available from ISTE, please visit iste.org/resources.

About the Author

Mark Gura has been an educator for more than three decades. The former director of instructional technology of the New York City Department of Education, he began his career as a teacher, and spent 18 years in elementary and middle school classrooms in Harlem. More recently, he has taught graduate education courses at Fordham University, Touro College, and New York Institute of Technology. Gura was a staff and curriculum developer for NYC's Central Division of Curriculum and Instruction before being recruited to develop and administer the first citywide instructional technology program. He has written extensively on education for the New York Daily News, Converge, and a variety of other education magazines, and has written and published numerous books on education, including *Getting Started with LEGO Robotics* (ISTE, 2011), and *Teaching Literacy in the Digital Age* (ISTE, 2014).

Gura has spoken on the subject of instructional technology throughout the United States. He lives in Jupiter, Florida, teaching graduate teacher education courses online, as well as writing and podcasting there.

Acknowledgments

The author would like to acknowledge the following colleagues for their contributions to this book. The time, enthusiasm, and expertise they shared in the interviews you'll find interspersed throughout this book added to what I had to say immensely and is much appreciated. They are:

Michele Haiken

Joel Heffner

Brittany Howell

Jamie Kaspar

Melinda Kolk

Tim Needles

Erin Olson

Rose Reissman

CONTENTS

Introduction

I was a classroom teacher for 20 years before moving on to serve in district administration and later teach graduate level education courses at a variety of universities. Early on in my teaching career I worked as a visual art teacher (my first love and license area) at a school for youthful offenders, highly challenged and violent youth, in the Harlem neighborhood of New York City.

This high action experience represented not only a paycheck but, more important, my own real-world education in what is possible and worthwhile in art education. Over time I observed that many of the behaviors that continually got my students in trouble appeared to be reflex responses. In other words my students seemed often to be incapable of evaluating situations and creating an appropriate response with which to handle them.

From that point on, with the blessing of the school's director (thank you, John) I transformed my class from the classic middle school visual art course to a course in creativity, a class in which students reflected on the phenomenon of creativity and how it might be called forth to positively impact their lives. I was hooked on this challenge and have made it part of every phase of my four-decade-long career as an educator, including my seven years as director of instructional technology of New York City's public schools.

Fast Forward: We live and work in a period in which social, economic, and political realities demand that we innovate and create new responses to quickly evolving challenges. In part, these realities have been brought about by the technologies we have invented. But those same technologies, or new ones we continue to invent, also provide the solutions to the challenges we live with.

Creativity *Now!*

Recently, the *Boston Globe* newspaper ran a story about how an education professor at Boston College has been engaged by education officials in China to help integrate more creativity into school curricula there. The Chinese Ministry of Education feels that teachers should engage students in new ways so the country can build a better workforce (Landergan, 2015). In an article in the *Globe and Mail* (a Canadian newspaper) titled "How do Finnish kids excel without rote learning and standardized testing?" Pasi Sahlberg, a Finnish education official, points out that the Finnish school system has engaged in redesigning learning according to how innovation occurs. They have begun to emphasize collaborative work and see knowledge as more than merely a cumulative store of objective information. "It is not primarily what individuals know or do not know, but more what are their skills in acquiring, utilizing, diffusing, and creating knowledge that are important for economic progress and social change," writes Sahlberg (Millar, 2013).

There are two important takeaways from these stories. First, the awakening desire to address how our schools have ignored and even discouraged students and teachers from working on developing student creativity is rapidly becoming a planetary drumbeat and call to action. Second, there is a body of knowledge already in place with which educators can address developing student creativity and innovation—one that represents a solid platform on which to expand professional knowledge and practice.

This second point is particularly important. As is indicated by a study released by Adobe in 2013, the state of creativity in education is not simply one of neglect; rather, the educational experience currently offered to our students actively discourages their growth as creative individuals, and testing and government mandates are stifling creativity in the classroom. The Adobe news release states, "This international study, 'Barriers to Creativity in Education: Educators and Parents Grade the System," shows there is a growing concern that the education system itself is a barrier to developing the creativity that drives innovation. Parents and educators agree that today's education system places too much emphasis on testing and not enough investment in the training, tools, and time needed to teach creativity (Adobe, 2013)."

Further, the situation isn't simply that educators must make the development of student creativity an important part of what they do, but that there is a good deal of urgency to this.

In an article in the magazine *Educational Leadership* titled "Why Creativity Now? A Conversation with Sir Robinson" the prominent British Education educator, Sir Ken Robinson, a popular campaigner for the reestablishment of creativity as a prime goal in schooling, states:

> We're living in times of massive unpredictability. The kids who are starting school this September will be retiring—if they ever do—around 2070. Nobody has a clue what the world's going to look like in five years, or even next year actually, and yet it's the job of education to help kids make sense of the world they're going to live in.
>
> You know, for my generation—I was born in 1950—we were told that if you worked hard, went to college, and got a regular academic degree, you'd be set for life. Well, nobody thinks that's true anymore, and yet we keep running our school systems as though it were. So many people have degrees now that an individual degree isn't worth a fraction of what it used to be worth. So being creative is essential to us; it's essential for our economy. (Azzam, 2009)

True, we are living and learning in technology dominated, digitally transformed times full of challenges. It's also true that the very same technologies that continue to cause disruption also represent opportunities for us to take the richness of life to the next level. The potential to do so is definitely there ... if only we can muster the requisite creativity. Thus, the urgency to understand creativity and to make it part of the education that all students are afforded is something that educators, and those who support them (supervisors, curriculum specialists, school administrators, parents, and others), *must* do. They must elevate creativity from the margins of the instructional program and place creativity at its very core where it can take its rightful place as one of the most important dimensions of modern education.

Why Aren't We Educating Innovators?

In our current dual pursuit of better educational outcomes and economic prosperity there is a crucial gap that seems to go unnoticed. I'm talking about the near total silence that exists concerning fostering creativity as a goal for our schools. This is true across the curriculum, including, and perhaps most perplexing, STEM (science, technology, engineering, and math) education, the area that so many look to for delivering important results that will help us cope with impending economic and environmental crises through innovation. But, if, as President Obama said, "Education is key to innovation," then why aren't we educating innovators?

In 2009 Mr. Obama announced his $260 million Educate to Innovate Campaign for Excellence in STEM Education, the goal of which he explained is "to move American students to the top of the pack in science and math achievement over the next decade (White House, 2014)." More recently, at the White House Science Fair, the president celebrated some truly exceptional work presented by the cream of our student population. But beyond good feelings engendered by this event, and promises of massive amounts of corporate money to be thrown at raising test scores in math and science, what precisely is going to be done to foster innovation? How will any of this actually produce the large cohort of creative, innovative, out of the box STEM thinkers that we must have?

Rather than simply buying in to pep rally hoopla, we need to ask some probing questions. There is too much at stake to skip vetting blue sky assertions. Principally, will continuing to educate our students in the same curriculum, only more effectively due to increased importance ascribed and greater funding committed, make a difference in terms of real world outcomes?

Our science standards, one road map that plots where we may actually arrive if all this money and attention get our education system moving faster, suggest the answer is "No!" Granted, these standards are brilliant documents that represent the work of many of our best science educators. But they are heavily invested in producing students who are knowledgeable *about* science: students steeped in facts, concepts, historical milestones, and understandings about the role of science. These standards are not, however, directed at producing students who are ready to innovate.

True, the standards stress abilities as well as content knowledge, the ability to do scientific inquiry being one notable skill set. However, a student who achieves to a high degree in relation to our science standards, although educated to be a knowledgeable citizen, an informed consumer, and a workplace participant who is comfortable with science, will not be a graduate ready to take his place among those who develop new energy sources, engineer higher protein crops, or develop approaches to banking that will enable more of the world's disenfranchised to pull themselves out of poverty. At best, we are educating a cohort of graduates qualified to assist and support those who will actually create the solutions, inventions, and next level approaches that will make our world more livable. But why aren't we educating to directly produce innovators?

Realizing Obama's goal to move American students from the middle to the top of the pack in science and math achievement may make us feel good, and may earn some political capital for those on whose watch it happens; but what will it accomplish in terms of actually getting our society to where it needs to go? That nations like Singapore, Sweden, South Korea, and The Netherlands produce higher test scores than the United States may be a blow to our ego, but will reversing this produce graduates who will help find a way to reduce arterial plaque? Or develop an inexpensive storage battery for an electric vehicle? Or find a way to reclaim potable water in areas where industry has fouled it? Just what is it that is on those tests that relates to populating our workforce with the people who will be able to do the things that count most, things that require innovation in STEM fields?

Granted, innovators in the sciences, business, even in social services can only benefit from a solid grounding in our current curriculum. The point, though, is that we can no longer afford to stand back and admire how well we have provided this grounding, while counting fully on some unidentified, wild card factor to inspire a small percentage of those educated this way to percolate up as innovators of tomorrow's inventions and solutions to problems. We are on the doorstep of a period in which producing innovators and envelope pushers has to become a principal goal of our educational system. Simply doing a better job at what we are currently doing is not a strategy that can achieve this!

We are moving away from an era in which graduates who are informed and competent are sufficiently prepared to make a difference in the world. Instead, we are entering a period of constant, rapid, and profound change in which innovation and creativity are increasingly more important. Educating our students more intensely in a curriculum designed for success in the previous era won't help us produce the people we need now and in the future. We need to educate in a way that fosters creativity.

I am not talking about simply reinstating arts programs in our schools. While the arts obviously are related to creativity, they will not necessarily help us develop truly creative students—students who are innovative in the ways they'll have to be. Our goal as educators must be to produce reflective creators who understand the mental processes behind their creativity and how they can be applied to other situations, problems, and challenges beyond the context of the arts.

Can creativity be taught? There is indeed a body of research and practice that shows it can. But what needs to be done is much more complex than simply adding a new class to our course load. Our overall curriculum doesn't need to be scrapped and rewritten wholesale. But it does need to be tweaked and refined with creativity as a new focus. More important, our schools need to be transformed into environments that encourage students to evolve and develop as creative individuals.

The harshest reality, though, is that not only are our schools not fostering creativity, but, as many like Sir Ken Robinson claim, they are actually discouraging it. A special edition of *Newsweek* magazine titled "The Creativity Crisis" agreed, giving suggestions about how creativity should be seen as a dimension of all curriculum areas, especially science (Bronson & Merryman, 2010). Galvanizing messages like these aside, where in our broad-based discussion about improving education is the goal of fostering creativity?

Are we stuck in habitual ways of looking at education that ensure disaster in the not too far off future? It would seem so. On the one hand, President Obama, among others, informs us of the overwhelming need for our educational system to produce innovators. On the other, we continue to avoid facing the need to map in detail precisely how we'll accomplish that. True, we'll have to explore some unfamiliar and uncomfortable territory to make the changes needed to significantly foster creativity in our schools. But that's not something that stops innovators.

How to Use This Book

This book will support educators in establishing an instructional practice that will encourage and support the development of student creativity. In essence, four varieties of things essential to fostering student creativity are presented: understandings about creativity and how it can be developed; establishing a creativity-friendly learning environment; activities to support the development of student creativity; and digital resources that can support and facilitate student creativity. Embracing and adopting any of these will increase the creativity friendliness of the instructional program provided students in a classroom or school. However, if all four areas are adequately addressed, then the supportive nature of the program will be covered fully. Consequently, in moving toward developing a teaching practice calculated to address the need for students to develop and employ their creativity, educators can use these four elements as both a checklist and as a planning and development resource.

1. **Aha moments and understandings: Background on why educators must foster creativity, how to develop and encourage creativity.**

    Why is it crucial that our students develop their creativity? What varieties of creativity are important and how will they be applied in their lives both in and beyond school? Can creativity be taught and developed? Defining the goal: creativity, innovation, invention, problem solving, critical thinking, and so on.

2. **Conditions: Classroom culture, teaching context, learning environment, and so on.**

    How does the creativity-friendly classroom differ from the traditional classroom? What sorts of rituals, traditions, agreements, and ways of being need to be in place for a classroom to support and encourage the development of student creativity?

3. **Activities: Descriptions of activity types and activity elements.**

    What sorts of activities nourish and support the development of student creativity? What elements do they have in common?

4. **Resources: An annotated listing of powerful digital tools and resources that can support the development of student creativity.**

    Which sorts of software, apps, and other digital resources are available and can be applied to nourishing and supporting students as they develop creativity? How can educators understand available resources in terms of broad categories, particularly in relation to the functions they provide?

PART 1

Understanding
CREATIVITY

"The value of nothing: Out of nothing comes something."

—Amy Tan (from her TED Talk, "Where Does Creativity Hide?")

What is creativity? Can it be taught? How do educators approach this subject when forming their practice? In this section, the phenomenon of creativity is examined in detail. Chapter 1 defines creativity and looks at how it relates to education. Chapter 2 looks at creativity and success, and explores why creativity is so vital to foster success in today's classrooms. Chapter 3 shows different sides of the creative process and frameworks for teaching creativity. Chapter 4 looks at innovation and problem solving as they relate to creativity.

Chapter 1

What Is Creativity…and Can It Be Taught?

In the *Business News Daily* article titled "Who Says Creativity Can't Be Learned?" Dr. Tina Seelig, Professor of the Practice in the Department of Management Science and Engineering at Stanford University, defines creativity as "the process of generating new ideas" explaining, "It is particularly important in industry because the world is changing incredibly quickly, and breakthrough ideas are required to stay competitive ….There is no one path to creative ideas, just as there isn't one way to get from San Francisco to São Paulo. However, there are ways that are easier than others. We can make the pathways to innovation much smoother by teaching people specific tools and techniques." (Smith, 2012)

In the video "Can Creativity Be Taught?" Sir Ken Robinson states, "Creativity is the process of having original ideas that have value …. It' a process … it's rarely the case if you are working on a creative project that you get the exact final version on your first attempt … it's normally a process of trial and error …. We know quite a bit about that process and how it works …. Secondly it's about original thinking … it doesn't have to be original to the whole world, but it's original to you …. Thirdly, it's about value …. All creative processes involve evaluation, making judgements …. There's often an early stage to it, when you're brainstorming, hypothesizing, but then it's work, it's crafting, it's trying again and trying to get it right." (Robinson, 2014)

Looking at the phenomenon of creativity through the lens represented by the two previous statements, educators will understand that it is something that can be taught, and that it is a known and understood way of working in our world. Further, creativity can be, to a sufficient degree, predictable and calculated, something that will continue to be more and more essential in a world in which original responses and solutions must be generated and applied to the stream of previously unencountered challenges that comprise life in the digital age.

Based on this understanding—one that embraces the dual reality of both possibility and necessity—educators will have to analyze what they currently provide students and strategize how to transform it so that, among other outcomes, students understand creativity and see how they can make it part of their own repertoire of learning and working, in school and beyond.

In short, students should be comfortable and confident in responding to prompts from their teachers, or to prompts they generate on their own as part of activities and experiences guided by their teachers, that call for creative responses. They should understand approaches and techniques for generating original ideas (these might range in type and character from solutions to practical problems expressed verbally or in text, to images or passages of poetry, to designs for machines or structures, and so forth). They should understand how to, and be comfortable in, selecting ideas appropriate to challenges and in developing those ideas by following practical processes to the point of reasonable completion and application. They should understand how to explain their creative decisions and process, and then present the product of their creative work to an appropriate audience. They should understand the creative process as one of ongoing improvement in which testing and evaluating their work is embraced and feedback, including feedback from an audience responding to their presentation of a final version, is collected and accepted and made the basis for "next step" creative work.

Creativity: The Goal

What do we want for our students? How do we want to prepare them for life in an ever more challenging world? Certainly we want to educate them, but what outcomes of that education will serve them as individuals and will serve our society as a whole?

Over the past few decades we have experienced sweeping changes in the way we learn, communicate with one another, and apply information to our problems and challenges. We've woken up to problems, many of them of life and death importance, that we hardly had an inkling existed. Bearing down on us are global warming, a ballooning national debt, drug resistant diseases, and the like. We've gone from an economic system that promised to many a lifetime of employment and a secure retirement, to one in which jobs last simply as long as they do. Employees then move on to the next job—or start their own business—as the fates of companies, in fact entire industries, rise and fall like the tide.

Our students will need to meet these challenges and many more, some of them more difficult than those we are currently aware of. How are we going to prepare them for this?

Do today's curriculum, standards, and commonly implemented instructional activities develop the creativity skills and understandings that will truly and fully serve our students? I think any honest reflection on the situation will produce an answer of "No!" In fact, I will add that the development of student creativity hardly appears on the typical school's radar screen. Quite likely there are a few spots in the instructional program that the average educator might point to as covering this crucial dimension of learning: "There are word problems in math and visual art and music classes, right?"

These will be discussed later on in this book, but no, these few spots are far from sufficient. I should add that instructional programs don't necessarily develop creativity unless they are targeted to do so.

Most important, in reflecting on and planning for the good work they do as instructors, educators may ask themselves, "Are my students learning the bodies of information they need to know? Are they acquiring the understandings they'll need and the sets of skills they'll have to be able to perform?" But how much of this essential professional reflection includes "Has my students' creativity been developed sufficiently?" I'm afraid it's a question that, which although crucial, is not even asked very often, let alone answered in the affirmative.

There are two pieces of especially good news here, though, that this book will deliver. One is that creativity can, in fact, be developed. And two, with the variety of technology resources currently available, doing so is not only possible, but practical and effective.

Creativity: Mission of the New Digital Learning Environment

A number of years back in a little spurt of inspiration and curiosity I decided to see what the National Science Education Standards, a toweringly powerful and influential document for many years, had to say about bringing the learning and development of creativity to the experience of science education. This was easy to do because the document, which is still available online by the way, is searchable digitally. I was surprised and dismayed to discover that thick document, one that functioned as our primary road map for what students should learn and be able to do in the area of science for well over a decade, had but a handful of references to creativity, and all of them tangential at that. To paraphrase them, they indicated that students should bring some creativity to their science activities, but gave almost no indication of how this should be achieved. Reflecting on this situation, I realized this squared with my overall experience of teaching and observing what countless teaching colleagues did in their classrooms.

Simply stated, schools and those who work in them or who support or influence them from the outside, have rarely paid much attention or put much effort into actually addressing the issue of how to ensure that our students develop their creativity and graduate as creative individuals who understand this most important and impactful aspect of human experience.

This, despite the fact that one often hears policy makers, from the president of the United States to the secretary of education on down to the mayors of our cities and the superintendents of schools and their staffs under them, overtly state their belief that our nation and society needs its schools to produce the next generation of innovators and creators. People in such positions often opine about how the key to our continued and future prosperity, security, and well-being hinges on us producing graduates who can take on challenges and come up with remarkable new solutions by exercising their creativity. Those of us who are intimately familiar with what actually is targeted and achieved within our schools, however, know that creativity simply hasn't been a direct goal—certainly not to any appreciable extent. Creativity is certainly not something that's often found its way onto the extended, communal "radar screen" of what's important to focus on.

In fact, it's probably true (as my own experience of working at every level in our nation's largest school system has clearly shown me) that educators at every level do not truly understand how creativity might be addressed by schools. If anything, when pressed they are likely to state that arts classes are the way to develop student creativity. This just before they lament that there are very few such classes offered any longer. But while there is some truth in this, it is not a fully accurate assessment at all. As a former visual art teacher, something I did for years on the way to becoming the director of instructional technology for the NYC Department of Education, I can tell you that while arts classes can be good incubators for student creativity, they won't do that unless they are specifically taught with that goal in mind, not something we can take for granted. Above all, we should be aware that all subject areas relate strongly to creativity. Science, social studies, language arts, music, and visual arts will not provide an adequate education to our students unless this important aspect of human learning is addressed.

Finally, we are at a perfect moment to do just that. The ways that knowing, learning, and communicating have evolved due to the emergence and near-ubiquitous adoption of digital technologies very strongly offers us a rich body of opportunity to finally make creativity a focus for our work with young learners. These technologies elevate the experience of the average learner today to one in which talent, steep skills learning curves, and elaborate materials and work environments are no longer barriers for developing creativity and applying it to solve problems and expand horizons.

Equipped with readily accessible technology resources, challenged with relevant prompts and activities, and guided by informed teachers who understand the phenomenon of creativity and the creative process and how it is fostered, supported, and applied, the average student can reasonably be expected to exhibit significant creativity throughout his or her school career and on into the world beyond school. This book will inform those wise enough to take on this essential work, providing insight, resources, action items, and hopefully some inspiration to that end. Let's create!

Creative, but How?
What Sort of Creativity Are We Talking About?

Throughout history remarkable individuals have been described as "creative." The image that is conjured up by this term often connotes a lone genius, like Archimedes; a lone eccentric—often an outcast—like Vincent van Gogh; or a brilliant pariah, like Thomas Edison, perhaps the greatest inventor in history and an individual who was branded as incapable of learning by his public school teachers. Certainly, these are inspiring individuals to whom we owe a great deal, but do they offer us an archetype of the creative individual on whom our schools should have our young people model themselves?

Figure 1.1: A 16th-century conceptual illustration of Archimedes having his "eureka" moment in the bath

One of the most compelling stories about creativity is that of Jules Henri Poincaré (1854–1912), the great mathematician, engineer, and philosopher of science who made many original fundamental contributions to pure and applied mathematics. Writing about the genesis of one of his breakthrough theories he explained:

> The changes of travel made me forget my mathematical work. Having reached Coutances, we entered an omnibus to go some place or other. At the moment when I put my foot on the step the idea came to me, without anything in my former thoughts seeming to have paved the way for it, that the transformations I had used to define the Fuchsian functions were identical with those of non-Euclidean geometry. I did not verify the idea; I should not have had time, as upon taking my seat in the omnibus, I went on with a conversation already commenced, but I felt a perfect certainty. On my return to Caen, for conscience' sake, I verified the result at my leisure.

What Poincaré describes here is one of the classic types of creative breakthrough experiences associated with genius. After intense, applied concentration and effort the creator turns his attention to something else, putting his work aside to focus on other, easier things. And then … without warning or any foreshadowing that it was about to happen, seemingly out of nowhere the object of his quest presents itself.

Such stories are fascinating and perhaps to some, inspiring, as well. Further, these can function as good content to share with students as part of a study about creativity. One good source for more of these stories is the article "AHA! Great Moments in Creativity" by Mitchell Ditkoff, which appears on the website Idea Champions (www.ideachampions.com). One anecdote related is that of Mozart, quoted as saying, "When I am, as it were, completely myself, entirely alone, and of good cheer—say traveling in a carriage or walking after a good meal, or during the night when I cannot sleep; it is on such occasions that my ideas flow best and most abundantly."

No doubt our society will continue to produce new Archimedes, van Goghs, and Edisons, and we will be enriched by their emergence and the work they do. However, it is very useful for us to reflect on how we hope to impact the average "every student" in terms of creativity, and define and understand in what ways today's participant in society should be creative.

Figure 1.2: A NASA team studying conceptual successors to the Hubble and the James Webb space telescopes

These stories of famous innovators describe a sort of creativity that is difficult to develop and not truly the sort of creativity that is of use for most of the situations and contexts in which students and graduates will need to be creative. Rather than creativity being understood as an anomalous work style of a rare segment of the population who are plugged into a mysterious source of wonder, what's of import to students and teachers today is creativity as a somewhat calculated, predictable response to a need or problem. It's a way of generating new things in a social setting that features work accomplished in groups and that embraces expertise from outside sources and feedback from others. In establishing this, today's educators may look to organizations like NASA, Apple, and Google that have become icons of contemporary creativity. Organizations like these provide models on which the education of today's students can be made relevant, in terms of supporting and developing creativity. After all, we are preparing many students to take their place in such workplaces down the road. In the *Fast Company* article "How to Design a Collaborative Environment Steve Jobs Would Approve Of," author Jeffrey Rodman explains that Jobs "knew how to design devices, no doubt about that. But Steve Jobs's talent for making user-friendly, intuitive technology didn't end at the iPhone. He had a gift for helping people interact as well, which is central to understanding the modern office and workplace of the future." (Rodman, 2014) It follows that students will need to learn how to function in such environments. Thus, the learning experiences we provide for them should be planned for that.

The Apple Classrooms of Tomorrow (ACOT2) website states:

> Innovation is the fuel that drives the global economy and it must be fostered in our nation's schools. Business leaders recognize that the new competitive frontier in the world of work is place-based innovation—the ability to innovate again and again within one environment. What this means for education is that learning, creativity and innovation skills are critical to future success in life and work and should be an integral part of a 21st century curriculum …. Those who have successfully created cultures of innovation and creativity suggest that one key is to abandon efficiency as a primary working method and instead embrace participation, collaboration, networking, and experimentation. This does not mean that focus, process, and discipline are not important; just that innovation and creativity require freedom, disagreement, and perhaps even a little chaos—especially at the beginning. (Apple Inc, 2016)

However, it's not enough for us to agree that we want to develop student creativity and turn out graduates who can accurately be described as "creative." Creative, as a description is too general. In fact, describing our goal in such simple terms speaks to our lack of understanding about what we actually mean by the word and more to our feeling of the unattainable aspect of it. Some of the ways that individuals function as creators in the evolving intellectual environment and professional world are described below. Coping with the demands and challenges of the 21st Century requires students to become creative in the following ways.

Creative as part of a team. An individual who is capable of and comfortable with being creative collaboratively, alongside other members of a team or an extended group.

Creative as a natural reaction to life's and work's common needs. An individual who confidently holds creativity as a principal and favored way to respond to needs and situations as they arise.

Creative in response to a focused challenge. Someone able to generate original, innovative ideas that address specific needs for creativity, directly.

Creative in identifying and articulating relevant problems. An individual who is adept at and comfortable with identifying challenges to tackle that are relevant and appropriate.

Free of preconceived notions. An individual who is creative in the sense of solving problems with fresh thinking and responses.

Reflectively creative. Someone who is aware of the creative process and directs it as part of the experience of creativity and its application.

Creative in intellectual common spaces. An individual who is creative in forums and on the web inviting co-creators, audience, and sources of feedback.

If we are to produce students who are creative in relevant, impactful ways, then our program to develop that skill set must be calculated to generate that result. Simply planting a seed and watering it is not enough focus or support.

INTERVIEW
Melinda Kolk

Melinda was a founder of Tech4Learning, a company dedicated to creating student multimedia tools for the classroom with a particular eye toward broad-based adoption so that a very high percentage of teachers opt to use them with their students. Ms. Kolk is currently Editor in Chief of *Creative Educator* magazine.

MG: Tech4Learning is an organization that has done a good deal toward promoting the common classroom use of digital resources to support and promote student creativity. Please share a bit about its focus and the things it hopes to accomplish.

MK: The efforts of Tech4Learning, as have evolved over the years, are most strongly directed at helping teachers engage students in activities to teach content and skills within the core content subject areas in ways that are more open and creative. Not necessarily developing student creativity for its own sake, but as a means to get kids to go deep with the required content. A creative approach is much more exciting for students and their teachers, too. I like the term "design thinking," which is a marriage between analytical thinking and creative thinking—we've not always been good with divergent, creative thinking.

MG: How do learning activities that encourage students to access and tap their creativity affect important learning?

MK: Creativity lets us really build our ability to ask questions, rather than come up with what the answers should be or what we think others think the answers should be. Giving kids the freedom and encouragement to ask questions for the sake of asking good questions is important. I can see that a kid might raise his hand to ask a big question, and he might get a response from a teacher that that's not what the lesson is about just then. I'm sorry, but that's what that kids need to think about right now. It gives us a window into how they are understanding the world, what their interests are. So giving kids something open-ended, an idea for a potential investigation, that doesn't have an obvious right answer—that's the sort of thing that we need to offer more of. Or it might be a tool that's open-ended or an attack that's open-ended, something that rewards risk taking, that rewards passion in interest, that rewards that kind of tangential thought process—those are important invitations to kids. But these are things that we need to explore much further in education.

I don't think developing student creativity and tapping their creativity as an approach to have them achieve targeted learning goals is something that can be accomplished by simply dedicating scheduled blocks of time for it. On the other hand, we could increase student creativity every single day, every single minute by doing things like rewarding risk taking, asking open-ended questions, perhaps by not asking questions—letting there be a silence, and letting the students fill it by asking their own questions.

Building in time for wonder would help—we've pretty much squashed curiosity out of things. We insist on kids learning the research process instead of just exploring things. The amount of things we are responsible for as teachers is growing, and there's a lot of pressure from the outside that makes it difficult to include things that develop creativity. Small wonder we don't know all that much about creativity—we don't really understand it. We kind of know creativity when we see it, but don't know how to cultivate it.

MG: For teachers who are now beginning to turn their focus to making creativity a student learning goal, and/or an approach to supporting students in meeting more traditional learning goals, what sorts of activities would you recommend?

MK: I think simple activities, like asking kids to come up with their own graphic organizers, are effective. Ask them to draw a graphic organizer or challenge them to think about the way graphic organizers represent things and asking them if they can think of a way that might work better. Perhaps simply to examine a number of graphic organizers and to figure out which features they like and to combine them in some new way that works for them. Involve them in an effort in which the process is more important than the content and the product. So, the time and place to introduce creativity into student activity is during the process of doing anything.

_____

MG: Where do you see teaching and learning that embrace student creativity—both as a goal and a platform for a freshened-up understanding of learning—taking us?

MK: In making all this the new classroom reality, we have made some important shifts. I see, for instance, in teaching math, at least in the early grades, that we are not so solely focused on arithmetic functions, but on understanding, and that involves students having their own body of multiple understandings that they express in a personal way. It's all about teachers choosing to focus either on the right answer or on the right question. And do we see students' imaginative questions as interruptions into the lessons that have been planned, or as opportunities to explore the curriculum in new ways? Hopefully, the latter is gaining increased respect. Teachers need to develop the habit of thinking creatively about instruction and student responses, and as a result the culture of their classrooms will offer opportunities for students to develop their creativity.

_____

MG: Tech4Learning is a provider of resources that have resonated deeply for many teachers. How would you characterize its resources?

MK: Tech4Learning provides tools that can be seen as a blank canvas, a digital multimedia composing platform.

_____

Melinda described to me the type of creativity-focused project she appreciates. This might be something like a storybook created by the students with the teacher stipulating that the student should start by writing a paragraph that contains at least three facts about an animal that he or she chooses to create a project about. The challenge might offer a focus like, "Now that you've chosen an animal and have found out some information about it, create a zoo enclosure for this animal that would make the animal happy and allow people to visit it. What would it look like? How would people interact with it? What do the animals need to have in it?" The teacher might add that the storybook the student creates should have images with labels that the student creates. Perhaps it should also contain photos that the student finds. The teacher might create a list of suggestions and stipulate that the students each address a specific number of things on the list as they do their storybook project. And of course, the teacher might let the student choose the format of the project, as well. So, in addition to a storybook, they might do a poster or a brochure or something else.

Chapter 2

Creativity
and Success

Today's workers, entrepreneurs, and world citizens are required to be part of a creative team. Consequently, in addition to making the development of student creativity a goal of our classrooms, a related goal is to inculcate in students the methodology and culture of creativity found in the digital-age workplace.

Among other ideas and beliefs that today's students will need to explore is an understanding of the place and value of creativity in the workplace and other institutions that impact life. This is a new focus for schools and students. The *Huffington Post* article "Creativity and Innovation: Your Keys to a Successful Organization" is emblematic of this new view of work and success in the digital age, stating:

> The companies that have done the best over the long haul are those who are the most creative and innovative. These organizations don't copy what others do; instead, they may use innovative ideas from others as a spring board to come up with a unique application, product, or service for themselves. They tend to distance themselves from the competition rather than compete with them. If they see another company copying what they do, they create something new and better. In other words, they are able to leverage their creativity and their innovative capabilities to attain long-term success. (Burrus, 2013)

The Need to Be Creative

In the article "Creativity Is the Key Skill for the 21st Century," Dr. Mark Batey, joint chair of the Psychometrics at Work Research Group at the Manchester Business School of the University of Manchester, states:

> Against a backdrop of uncertainty, economic turmoil, and unprecedented change a new picture is emerging of the skills and traits for success (and perhaps even simply survival) in the modern era. At the heart of this essential skillset for the future lies ... creativity. A raft of recent research studies demonstrates that creativity is vital from the shopfloor to the boardroom and at the level of the individual to the organization as a whole. What is more ... our economic fortunes at a societal level probably rest on creativity too. (Batey, 2012)

Batey lists seven themes and related research studies that verify, amplify, and explain this assertion:

1. Creativity and innovation are the number one strategic priorities for organizations the world over.

2. Creativity is part of all our day jobs.

3. Organizational profitability rests on individual creativity.

4. Creative teams perform better and are more efficient.

5. Creative organizations are more profitable.

6. Creative leadership is fundamental.

7. Successful economies and societies will need to be creative.
   (Batey, 2012)

Much of this represents far more than simple justification for making creativity an important goal of instruction. It represents a body of thought that our students would do well to learn as part of the big picture understanding that emerges from the aggregation of ideas they learn over the course of their education.

INTERVIEW

Joel Heffner

Joel Heffner is a social studies teacher and instructional technology specialist.

MG: How do we bring creativity into social studies class?

JH: Thinking of things I've done in the classroom, let me give you my favorite example of creativity in social studies. I told the class that they would all make videos on a scene from American history as a special project. I let the students break up into small groups of three or four. I gave them a few weeks to accomplish the task. Students were expected to determine their own format. Despite questions from students about grading, they were informed that the project would be ungraded. All students did the project and did it well. In fact, it may well have been the best activity ever done in the history of the school.

One great example of a video some of the kids came up with was on the Triangle Shirtwaist Factory fire disaster. It featured the group dressing up one of its boys in a dress standing on a fire escape and yelling about a fire inside. In the next scene you see him jumping out the window. Of course, they actually had a manikin that they put the same dress on and threw that out the window and the scene concluded with the boy on the ground, apparently dead from his fall out of the window to escape the fire. It was a powerful video.

Another group's video was a battlefield scene from the American Revolution. Near the school was a golf course, and these kids' video showed them hiding among sand traps and bunkers restaging an actual historic battle. It was very effective, and through doing these projects those kids probably learned more about the particular events in history they chose than they would have had they been taught from the textbook and library research. My conclusion was that the creativity will happen and be applied to the learning the teacher hopes for if you give students an assignment, of course with some guidelines, and let them figure out how to do it the best way for them. And of course my thought about this often was that the students would think, when they compared the two types of experiences, that they were getting away with something when they were really learning through creative projects. I understood that they were actually doing a great deal more than they would have to do in a traditional assignment, but—and this is crucial—they were having a good time doing the project. So long as the students' experience of a good time and my idea of what they should be doing and learning coincided, I was always satisfied as their social studies teacher.

MG: So basically what happened was that the students interpreted the teacher's challenge to report on an important event in American history by researching it and recreating it in a video through which others could learn about it, too.

JH: And now, such videos can be uploaded online and everyone can see them. And it gets easier to do such projects all the time. Smartphones have video cameras, so getting access to equipment isn't the issue it was in the past—although student research and ingenuity are still key needs. The creativity in the project only amplifies how students find their own way to important information.

One year I volunteered to teach social studies to a special education class (not my normal assignment), something that I found to be difficult. At one point I was going to teach this largely minority group about slavery and the Dred Scott Decision. Using technology I sent each student a letter made to look like it had been sent personally to them by Dred Scott himself. This resonated strongly and made this a special experience for them. Later, I had them respond personally to their letter. The nontraditional way that the facts had been presented to them sparked their creativity, and their responses were genuine and original.

You might take this approach and send students an email from Richard Nixon, or a tweet from Ulysses S. Grant.

When I first started teaching, I'd give an assignment that involved students in writing responses to my questions and, after the student had done it, it would end up in their notebook or desk and probably would never be considered again. Now student work can go on the web. I like simple-to-do, free resource-based, teacher-created websites. I like the Mozilla Sea Monkey Composer resource, personally.

The fact that the work will truly be seen by an audience, and that this audience may make comments, provides students with important motivation to produce something to be proud of. Student voice and choice is important in such web-based projects, so that even though students are staying within a general subject chosen by the teacher, they each choose their own specific area to study and express what they learn and want others to know about it in their own way. In other words, a teacher-defined challenge, but one that has enough flexibility in it so that each student can have a self-personalized learning experience.

Another project I did with my students that offers a good idea of the role of creativity in social studies is something that came out of a discussion I had with a class about a governor. At one point a student was wondering about what the state's governor would have to say about a subject the class was focusing on. My initial reaction was to assert that as a class we should find out. The class made up a body of questions, created a questionnaire based on them, and then sent them to the 50 U.S. governors. After a short while, we received a response from the governor of Maine. After sharing the response with the students, I began a posting at the head of the class a list of the governors who responded. The list continued to expand as responses rolled in one after the other. Eventually the students created a class publication that included our survey, quotes from the governors' responses, and our reactions to the experience—designed and formatted by the students as their own creation. This activity could be done with famous or non-famous individuals. Student parents are a ready-made subject, as their email addresses are easy to find.

MG: What advice do you have for teachers about the proper role of technology in learning projects that involve creativity?

JH: Don't look at the technology and try to figure out what you can do with it; ask yourself what you want to do, and then find a technology that can help you do it!

Chapter 3

The Creative Process

So where do original ideas, visions, goals, and concepts come from? Yes, there is a mysterious side to it, but a good deal of practical experience has produced a body of predictable practice that can be applied to creativity within the common contexts of teaching and learning.

Apart from the variety of creativity that is described as spontaneous inspiration and insight, there is also creativity resulting from a calculated process. Process may be a departure from what many of us think of when we consider creativity. The classic understanding of creativity often includes accounts like the story of Archimedes in the bath when he is hit with a bolt-from-the-blue insight, to which he shouted "Eureka!" Such moments are unpredictable, undefinable, and unmanageable. However, there are other understandings and approaches for experiencing the creative process. For the development of student creativity, there are approaches by which creativity can be engaged. This process is not unlike that of a driver who puts an already running car into gear in order to begin a journey. Once teachers understand and bring their teaching in line with practical approaches for engaging creativity, the prospect of fostering creativity comes into focus as something that is doable, manageable, and predictable.

Frameworks to Facilitate Creativity and Its Development

Many teachers are already familiar with the writing process, a framework and procedure by which the act of writing, including creative writing, can be approached so that all students can succeed at it. Using the writing process, students are supported in creating essays and stories, and do so in a way that requires only a reasonable stretch. We can use the writing process, along with a number of other, related creative process formats to better understand the process of creativity in general, as well as to select and utilize procedures and tools for use with students.

Beyond seeing these process formulas as individual frameworks, though, it is useful to see what they have in common. Doing so can shed light on the general prospect of creativity and can help foster it, powerfully.

Stages of the Creative Act

The act of creativity can be generalized, and such a generalized understanding reveals that the act of creativity takes place in stages. Of course, the construct represented here is somewhat artificial because the stages are viewed as being entirely separate and distinct. This likely is an exaggeration done for the sake of illustration. My own creative process, something I've pondered considerably, includes degrees of blending of the stages, which may happen out of the strict sequence indicated.

Nonetheless, the sequence can be seen as composed of the following steps:

- An initial stage in which the challenge, at least in an early, conceptual state is identified and tentatively articulated

- An incubation stage in which the early concept develops beyond the initial set of ideas

- An insight stage in which the evolving form of the creative product or solution itself informs the creator about possible and appropriate further development

- An elaboration phase which sees the creator fully developing the product or solution, perhaps taking it through various and repeated sub stages of refinement

- An expressive phase in which the product or solution is made ready for and then shared with an audience or users

- Finally, a review phase in which the success or failure of what's been produced is analyzed and determined. This last phase may be extended or lead to another phase in which a following project is conceived based on the one just completed.

While this list identifies many common elements to creative work and procedures, as we will see there are more specific creative process formats. And, of course there are many variations on those, as well. Table 3.1 offers a representation of the creative process shared by Marvin Bartel, art instructor at Goshen College.

The Writing Process

Many variations of the writing process have been developed and implemented over the years. In its most common form it involves the following five steps: pre-writing, drafting, revising, editing, and publishing.

This common process format is designed to carry a creative effort through from generalized, somewhat undefined beginning ideas to a clearly finished version that is intended to be shared and appreciated by audiences. The pre-writing stage may

Table 3.1: Stages of the Creative Act

PERCEPTIVE STAGE	INCUBATION STAGE	INSIGHT OR ILLUMINATION STAGE	ELABORATION STAGE	EXPRESSION STAGE	EVALUATION OR VERIFICATION STAGE
Identify and focus the issues Play around Listen Take in ideas List things Decide on limits Clarify problem Give up, but expect to succeed	Subconscious mind working No real time used Doing other things Relaxed	You expect it to happen, but you don't know when	Develop it, apply skill and knowledge	Finalize it Make it convincing Authenticate it Patent it Copyright it Publish it	Ask, does it work? Is it beautiful or elegant? Does it help people? Does it make a profit? Is it better than before?

include numerous things, including personal idea generation (for a subject, theme, or topic), in which the individual formulates, or perhaps even free associates, responses to prompts and or brainstorms. This work generates a great many possible choices, and the writer knows and understands that there is no risk or commitment involved because these may all be discarded as he pleases.

Stages of the Writing Process

There are many varieties of the writing process. However the following version with its five stages (plus one optional stage) is highly representative of the process and its common implementation.

1. **Pre-writing:** Before beginning to write students must plan. This can include researching or gathering information through non-library approaches, like interviewing, brainstorming, outlining, and storyboarding.

2. **Drafting:** This involves a first attempt at moving from gathering materials and ideas listed in an outline to creating a narrative format that can be recognized as a story, essay, article, or other form of writing.

3. **Revising:** After reviewing their draft(s) or receiving and reflecting on feedback from others about it, students make changes in format, content, and voice as part of an ongoing process that will continue until the finished product is reached.

4. **Editing:** As the drafts or ongoing versions of the piece are refined, students review and improve them with an eye toward the technical side of writing. These refinements may include flow and voice of the writing, as well as spelling, grammar, and punctuation.

5. **Publishing:** This final stage of the writing process involves sharing one's work with others. Current technology enables schools and their students to accomplish this in ways very similar to those of professional publishers. Publishing online greatly facilitates the reach of sharing to a broader audience beyond the classroom. Further, online publishing using resources like blogs makes it easy for readers to provide feedback through a "comments" feature.

6. **Optional step for writing projects:** This extra step, which teachers may or may not choose to make a formal part of the writing initiative in their classrooms, involves building on writing projects already completed to launch students into further writing projects. This optional step makes writing an ongoing effort that is part and parcel of all explorations undertaken by students.

Through use of the writing process, students can come to understand that much of the creativity of writing can be managed and done with predictable success. The following stages of the process model demonstrate how a rough and generalized body of ideas can be processed, worked on, refined, and clarified such that a unique and effective original product is produced.

Technology to Support the Writing Process

Some technology tools commonly used to support the process of writing include spelling/grammar/punctuation checking software, graphic organizers, and outlining and storyboarding resources. Search engines can be used to find and support examples, references, and illustrations. Online collaboration resources enable students to work on a project both in and beyond the classroom. Finally, resources like Google's Blogger platform (blogger.com) and the issuu (issuu.com) online book publishing resource enable students to present their work.

Using technology students can create unlimited copies of a draft or version. This allows for a number of great advantages. Among them:

- Students may easily move phrases, sentences, and whole paragraphs around within their draft, easily trying different possibilities but without great effort. Doing this without technology would be labor intensive and could discourage revision work.

- Students may develop their draft in a number of different ways without losing the original state of a draft. Thus, they may review, compare, and select their choice from a number of versions. This a great advantage in helping students understand how a given piece will "read" to their audience.

- Teachers may "mark up" student work digitally in ways that can be removed by the student as they move forward with their work.

- Technical issues, like spelling, grammar, and punctuation can be addressed through the use of digital resources that make reviewing and fixing problems relatively easy. While technology resources make this quick and user friendly, students still need to participate directly in the editing process by reflecting on problems and suggestions that the technology provides.

- Publishing is made possible and easy to accomplish through technology resources such as Blogger, Wordpress, and others. Publishing resources like these help students produce a professional looking product. These works can be published on the web, making it easy for students to reach either a focused or a broad audience, and (depending on how the teacher chooses to set the resource's preferences) collect feedback from readers through the "comments" function. Briefly, there are a couple of easy things that teachers should understand so as to make a general blogging resource secure for use in their school:

- Student work need not bear students' names in photos or reveal personal information or identities in order for their posted work to have impact and meaning.

- A class blog may suffice, precluding the need for each student to run his or her own individual blog. A class blog offers a great deal of learning value even if the teacher is the only one to actually upload or maintain the blog.

- Blog preferences can easily be set so that the teacher can review and accept or reject any comments submitted by readers.

- The blog format can be tweaked so that students viewing the blog are not enticed to examine other blogs not vetted by the teacher.

Resources for Writing Projects

There are many supportive resources to be found on the web. One good example is ReadWriteThink (readwritethink.org) which offers numerous interactive resources and tools that can help students accomplish a variety of goals—from organizing their thoughts to learning about language—all while having fun. Among the resources for teachers is a strategy guide for implementing the writing process (tinyurl.com/22novvv).

Another great resource for supporting student writers is the Purdue University Online Writing Lab, or OWL (owl.english.purdue.edu), which offers a great variety of writing ideas and suggestions for writing projects.

The Design/Engineering Process

Another formalized process (procedural framework) is the design/engineering process. Originally developed and implemented in engineering schools, it has been appropriated and applied to K–12 STEM learning, as well. Pondering the development of a mechanical or electronic machine, or other item of applied technology, may seem daunting to those who are uninitiated into thought tools like this. But using the design/engineering process will help demystify the creative process involved and empower students as they use it. Further, they can reflect on how it provides guidance and support while it remains flexible enough to allow for originality and inspiration.

The stages of the design/engineering process are:

- Identify problem

- Brainstorm

- Design

- Build – Test – Evaluate – Redesign (this is an ongoing stage that should continue until an optimum product or solution is reached)

- Share work with others (publish or present)

The design/engineering process framework takes students in a logical sequence through an approach that mimics the actual working process of engineers and inventors, from a notion to a focused challenge and on through development of a solution to the point where it is finished and ready to be presented and shared with the world.

Resources for the Design/Engineering Process

PBS did a fine job of explaining, illustrating, and presenting the design/engineering process to students in its half hour show *Design Squad Nation*: (tinyurl.com/yjomlwr). Many episodes can be found on YouTube (e.g., DSN ep: 1 Apache Skateboarders). PBS further supports teachers in embracing the show and its approach through interactive, online resources.

For an idea of an instructional context in which the design/engineering process framework is a natural and effective fit, see Suzie Boss's blog post on Edutopia, "Shoe Design Offers a Trojan Horse for Problem Solving with Design Thinking" (tinyurl.com/j9lkfre).

Another worthwhile resource for understanding the design/engineering process and its fit in instruction, even for elementary students, is the Museum of Science, Boston, website (eie.org/overview/engineering-design-process).

A good video to explain the design/engineering process to students was produced by NASA for Kids. See "Intro to Engineering" on YouTube (tinyurl.com/zsfxyjc).

A very useful (free downloadable PDF) poster for the classroom, or for student book covers and the like, is provided by The Works Museum (theworks.org/wordpress/wp-content/uploads/2013/03/Engineering-Design-Process.pdf).

For those looking for a connection between creativity and science, Table 3.2 provides valuable insight. It is also available in the free, downloadable PDF book

Engineering the Future: Science, Technology, and the Design Process–Teacher Guide from the National Center for Technological Literacy/The Museum of Science (tinyurl. com/hnqgdty).

Table 3.2: Connection between scientific and design processes

SCIENTIFIC INQUIRY	ENGINEERING DESIGN
Formulate a question	Define a problem
Research how others have answered it	Research how others have solved it
Brainstorm hypotheses and choose one	Brainstorm solutions and select one
Conduct experiment to test the hypothesis	Create and test a prototype
Modify hypothesis based on results	Redesign solution based on test results
Draw conclusions and write paper	Finalize design and make drawings
Communicate findings orally and in writing	Communicate design in words and drawings
Investigate new questions	Define new problems

Source: National Center for Technological Literacy/The Museum of Science, Boston

Visual Art Process

One further example of a creative process framework comes from my own life experience. As a young man I was very committed to becoming a successful visual artist. When I entered the work force, I took on the profession of public school visual art teacher, something into which I threw myself, bringing my experience as an artist as part of what I had to offer the students I worked with over many years. I had experienced a degree of success with my drawings and watercolors, showing in a number of galleries and selling a number of designs to limited edition print publishers. Still, when I worked on my art I was at a loss to understand why it was that sometimes I produced very successful paintings and at other times the results I produced fell far short of any standard I set for myself. Even with the level of success I had experienced, I decided to go back to square one and enrolled in the drawing class of Anthony Palumbo, held each Saturday at the Art Students League of New York in Manhattan. I ended up remaining one of Anthony's students for a good number of years. Anthony, a former student of the highly successful Burne Hogarth and Reginald Marsh, was a classically trained fine arts draughtsman of extraordinary ability and insight. Over the course of several years not only did my own drawing improve immeasurably, but the concepts I gleaned from Anthony's teachings and corrections of my work powerfully crept into my own teaching. In short, the process that I took away from Anthony's class may be understood as follows:

Exploration and Experimentation: Engage in a period of loose exploratory trials. During this phase of the creation of a work, using a noncommitted "searching" line, the purpose is to explore, not to make a defined statement.

Discovery and Refinement: From the myriad meanderings generated in the experimentation phase, select those passages and elements that suggest things to keep; gradually darken and sharpen lines that define those. As the image that is suggesting itself begins to coalesce, switch from a searching, experimental line to a "committed line" that communicates it is defining a specific image.

Definition, Declaration, and Commitment: As you continue with this process, elements not chosen, experiments whose function was to show where else to look for the final image, can be blurred, removed, or transformed into background. The elements you've kept, further defined, and committed to will be the core of your finished piece.

Table 3.3: Teaching the Creative Process: From Imagination to Innovation

RECOGNIZE	IMAGINE	INITIATE AND COLLABORATE	ASSESS	EVALUATE AND CELEBRATE
Becoming aware of a challenge or opportunity within a domain of interest Possibility thinking; problem finding Maintaining a healthy state of mind (alertness, attitude, brain health)	Applying thinking skills to develop ideas for solutions Learning to think flexibly between divergent and convergent processes Learning fluency and future thinking	Using process and design thinking Taking risks and learning to control behavior Working in a collaborative manner Learning and practicing interpersonal and leadership skills	Monitoring progress; sometimes requires starting over or admitting failure	Reflecting on the experience, resources, teamwork, and celebrating the solution

Source: www.destinationimagination.org/who-we-are/the-creative-process

Review and Finish: The above elements of the process: the phase of risk free, noncommitted exploration—the phase of selection of lines and elements to keep, to work with, and to commit to—and the final phase of full clarification continue until the results suggest that it has come as far as it can without detracting from the overall effect and message. In other words, the work is finished.

I went on to use this approach to produce many works of art with which I was fully satisfied, and I structured my teaching to reflect it as well, offering my students something rarely given, an actual method and approach through which they, in turn, could produce work that they believed in and were satisfied with.

Teaching the Creative Process

Clearly the approach taken by all of these processes offers insights into how students can be guided in developing creativity as they work on creative projects and efforts. We can extrapolate from these a general understanding of a conceptual creative process. In fact, Table 3.3, drawn from the Destination Imagination website (destinationimagination.org), is a valuable attempt to provide a generalized map of the Creative Process. It provides a sequential list of behaviors on which teachers can inform and plan activities for students.

Visualizing Innovation by Mapping its Process

While there is no definitive distinction between creativity and innovation (the two are interrelated—more on this in the following chapter) we often see innovation as applied and implemented creativity. To understand it, traditionally we focus on the effect, the application of a new developed product or tool, for instance. One example might be the load bearing roller, something that powerfully impacted the lives of people by enabling the construction of important monuments. Less commonly, we consider cause as well as effect. In the case of the roller, that cause may have been the need of ancient stone workers to move blocks of stone that were heftier than those previously carried or dragged into place. However, to fully understand Innovation, especially from the standpoint of supporting students in developing the body of skills they need to be innovative, mapping out a full process is very useful. The following is an easy to see and comprehend example.

In his online article "The Innovation Process" Jeffrey, Baumgartner, a writer and speaker on Innovation strategies for business and author of the book *The Way of the Innovation Master,* explains:

Figure 3.1 Elements and sequence of a creativity process. This is a generalized conception of a formally conceived process to guide and support creativity.

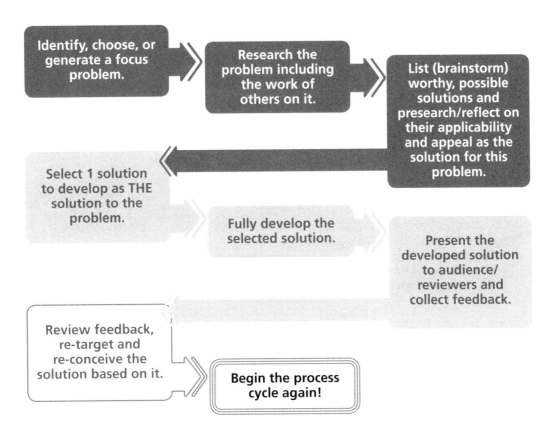

The innovation process, in the business context, is a structured action that is remarkably easy to implement. It begins with a problem and ends with profit. As such, it is the ideal business process. While intended to inform business, this process formula may be tapped by teachers for student creative projects as it embraces the basic elements of creativity in the context of institutional application. (Baumgartner, 2009)

Here are the steps in the process that Baumgartner outlines in his article:

1. Begin with a problem

2. Convert the problem into a challenge (a challenge is a short, terse question that invites creative solutions)

3. Challenge colleagues to suggest creative solutions

4. Collaborative idea generation

5. Combine and evaluate ideas

6. Develop ideas

7. Implement ideas

We've looked at the wide variety of conceptualizations and representations, above, of the creative act occurring within the specific contexts of separate disciplines like writing, visual art, and engineering. Still, opportunities to foster student creativity may be found outside contexts in which these specific varieties of process and their corresponding frameworks are a good match. To better understand the creative process, Figure 3.1 represents the essential elements in sequence.

INTERVIEW
Erin Olson

Erin is an instructional technology consultant with the Prairie Lakes Area Education Agency. She is a former middle school language arts and high school English teacher. Erin's work has been featured and discussed in the *New York Times* as well as on CNN News. She is the creator of the genius hour project Read, Be Inspired, Do Something Inspiring.

MG: How would you explain how learning activities in the area of creative writing can be part of developing student creativity?

EO: The opportunity to explore the world through another lens can be fostered through creative writing. Igniting imagination within our students happens with our intentional learning design. Engaging students in experiences where there is no one right answer, but there is possibility, is imperative.

MG: Can you give a good example of a learning activity that is directed at fostering student creativity?

EO: Take a picture of a concrete noun to symbolize an abstract noun. Write a poem to extend the connection, and photo edit the image to support the tone and mood you wish to convey. In this prompt, students are encouraged to see more than an object—to see all that it could symbolize. The writing provides opportunity for students to experiment with syntax and diction. There is no one right answer, but there is possibility.

My semester test in creative writing was simple: Give the gift of writing. Students amazed me with their ability to combine their talent, their learning, to a desire to honor another. Because they had experienced a semester filled with opportunity, the lack of parameter was not paralyzing, but a liberating call to make for a purpose.

MG: Can you share some examples of technology resources useful for teachers to foster students' creativity? And do you find that these are valuable in developing creativity?

EO: An often overlooked but powerful technology is the camera and photo and video editing apps and websites. Educators can include opportunities for students to show and share their creativity while meeting the demands of their curricular goals. Resources like the Connecting Creativity series from RethinkRedesign.org provide an opportunity for students to be creative. The series helps in the development of creativity by providing an idea. At the heart of every idea, students are the ones designing and developing, creating and contributing.

Social media avenues like Twitter have the potential to connect creators. All of us benefit from learning from those who are creative geniuses; it just makes sense for writers to gain inspiration from creative writers, engineers to gain inspiration from creative engineers, scientists to gain inspiration from creative scientists. . . . Implementing design thinking with an engineering model into learning experiences also supports creativity. Creativity is fostered through opportunity—opportunity to build, rebuild, design, redesign, construct, deconstruct, invent, reinvent. . . .Too often, creativity is not given the cognitive strength and power it deserves. This is more than coloring a tree pink. This is more than a refrigerator-worthy art project. The ability to see what has not been seen, the ability to create as simpler what has been made too complex, the ability to solve the unsolvable, design and redesign, and do all of this in a way that is original and collaborative. Creativity inspires and excites and can be nurtured. Connecting students to issues that need addressing and ideas that inspire genius helps nurture a desire to choose to be creative. Cultivating an environment where experimenting is encouraged and failure is expected as part of a learning process—that gives freedom to creativity.

Chapter 4

From Creativity to Innovation and Problem Solving

We can think of innovation as applied creativity. While a painter like Gauguin or Picasso might be satisfied with producing a unique image as an end unto itself, the innovator takes much the same impulse, process, and experience of bringing something new into focus, but with and for a larger purpose. Innovation is creativity that addresses the need for something new in an effort to solve a problem or to improve something. It is not solely the creation that matters, but its impact on the world and quality of life.

In other words, innovation is creativity applied appropriately and practically as an element in solving problems. It is one of the important skill sets and competencies that our graduates will need to have to succeed in the world they encounter when they graduate. Graduates well versed in these skills are what our society will continue to need for our continued survival, prosperity, and well-being.

Politicians, educational policy makers, and education administrators may state that our society needs more and more innovators and that our schools must address this need by turning out graduates who are familiar with and adept at the processes and skills associated creativity and innovation. However, the established culture of schooling more likely works against it.

Creating Innovators

In an eSchoolNews article titled "How—and Why—to Teach Innovation in Our Schools," Alexander Hiam, teacher and author of *Innovation for Dummies* and *The Manager's Pocket Guide to Creativity*, lists the following five dimensions of thinking as being essential to schools producing innovators: imagination, inquiry, invention, implementation, and initiative (Hiam, 2011).

Beyond simply agreeing with this, I'll add that, at least in part, educators might use this list as a bit of a reality check for evaluating the experience students have in their classrooms. I think any sincere asking of the question, "How prominent is the fostering of innovation skills currently in the typical school?" will produce the honest answer of, "Not much. We really should do much more."

These five elements represent entry points from which schools may conduct a more thorough and revealing self-analysis. Is student imagination truly encouraged and rewarded? If the school is intent on engaging students in activities through which it is hoped they memorize bodies of fact and simple skills routines so that they may recall and demonstrate them on tests simply for the sake of doing so, then the answer is most likely a resounding "No!"

In fact, in an environment where such dimensions of thinking and doing are uncommon, the opposite is likely the case and student imagination, a key element for innovation, will be seen as unproductive daydreaming.

Without imagination honored and encouraged, students will look for prescriptive direction from the teacher. Thus, inquiry may happen, but as required, prescribed, and already defined research assignments. True invention will not likely happen and implementation and initiative will, at best, be comprised of compliance with teacher-defined assignments.

Another example of worth comes from Thom Markham, a psychologist, school redesign consultant, and author of the *Project Based Learning Design* and *Coaching Guide: Expert Tools for Innovation and Inquiry for K-12 Teachers* (HeartIQ Press, 2012). In an article appearing on KQED's Mind Shift entitled "10 Ways to Teach Innovation," he states:

> We need to reinvent just about everything. Whether scientific advances, technology breakthroughs, new political and economic structures, environmental solutions, or an updated code of ethics for 21st century life, everything is in flux—and everything demands innovative, out of the box thinking. It follows that it is today's students who will have to handle all of this reinvention. Therefore, our schools should be preparing

them for that. Schools should be "putting curiosity, critical thinking, deep understanding, the rules and tools of inquiry, and creative brainstorming at the center of the curriculum. (Markham, 2013)

Unfortunately, this is very strongly not the case. If anything, the programs that are
valued in our schools and allocated the most attention, time, and resources represent the opposite end of the spectrum, and actually compete with those things that
would foster innovation skills and understandings in our students.

Markham, does, however, point out a number of ways that teachers can offer students the tools and experiences that spur an innovative mindset. He lists (among
others) these recommendations to teachers: teach concepts, not facts; reward discovery; make reflection part of the lesson; and be innovative yourself (Markham,
2013).

This is solid advice and no doubt educators would do well to institute these elements and dimensions of instruction as a major portion of the educational experience afforded today's students who must become the innovators of tomorrow.

Students Meeting the Challenge

What's crucial in all of this are the things students are challenged to do and produce. Currently, there are a number of programs that present real-world problems
to students of various ages, inviting them to wrap their brains around key problems
and come up with solutions. This book shares a list of such challenges, that may
serve as examples and models of this approach to engaging students to in finding
solutions to relevant, authentic, un-met needs, the type they see continually in the
news and beyond the classroom.

Here are some examples of what has resulted when students have been challenged
to apply their creativity to real-world problems. The examples come from among
dozens of student-developed innovations submitted to the IGNITE competition held
by the National Innovation Foundation of India.

- A pen to check concentration, with pressure sensors on the grip to indicate loss
  of concentration when the grip loosens. A student thought up this innovation
  based on his experience of not being able to concentrate during required reading at school.

- A ceiling fan with blades that fold down for easy cleaning. Switched off, the
  blades droop downward so they can be cleaned; and when switched on they
  become horizontal as in other ceiling fans.

- A low cost Braille printer from a modified dot matrix printer. The two student innovators once visited a school for the blind for a school project. There they saw that much of the printing work was done in a time consuming manual manner. Challenged by a teacher there, they came up with their own Braille printer using a dot matrix printer. (Pareek, 2014)

In 2012, one of the submissions to Microsoft's Imagine Cup—an annual event that "brings students together from across the world each year, in effort to use technology to solve the world's toughest problems"—was a navigation aide for the visually impaired. Worn on the head, the device emits sounds as the wearer approaches an object (Fox, 2012).

Another example of applied creativity is the Real World Design Challenge (realworlddesignchallenge.org), a national design competition for high school students with the goal of increasing the science, technology, engineering, and mathematics (STEM) workforce. In 2014, the Next Level team, representing South Burlington High School in South Burlington, Vermont, won the competition with its design of an unmanned system that improves precision agriculture through early detection of European corn borer infestations in corn fields (PTC, 2014).

Innovation Process

Clearly, teaching innovation, both the body of innovation-specific skills needed to be innovative and the body of understandings needed to make it part of one's intellectual repertoire can be made part of the instructional experience. How then can we best understand how to make this a broad-based effort so that all students everywhere can benefit from it?

Fortunately, there is both a framework to guide this sort of instruction, as well as endless opportunities for teachers to plan instructional activities that align this goal with required learning objectives in their subject areas, making for a convenient and appropriate fit.

Following is a basic structure for a simple innovation process that can accommodate a great many instructional goals and activity types. There are many innovation processes, and teachers should consider this one typical but not totally definitive. In other words, once comfortable with this approach, it may be modified to best suit the specific need and activity.

1. **Identify and define the focus problem.** Not only is this a logical starting place, but also it provides insight into the goal(s) of an effort and the indicators of success at the end of the process.

2. **Research the problem.** Research allows those working on the problem to understand the problem and reveal other attempts at solutions. It is very useful to know what has been tried already.

3. **List possible solutions (and evaluate them).** Ideas tend to come in packs. Identifying and describing one often results in more showing up. This step is crucial as the point in innovation (as opposed to pure, raw creativity) is to select the best, most practical solution and not simply to celebrate interesting and admirable possible solutions.

4. **Select a promising solution and develop it.** From the body of possible solutions that have been identified, the innovator(s) selects what seems to be the most promising and then does whatever is necessary to explain it to others and bring it to life.

5. **Apply the solution (implement, share, publish, elicit feedback, etc.).** Once the innovator(s) have developed and refined the solution to a sufficient point, they bring it into the world.

6. **Evaluate results, review feedback, and retarget and re-envision a better/ further solution.** Innovation is often an ongoing process. Solutions are (hopefully) interim solutions—that is, the best solution at the moment in an ongoing effort to address the problem. For instance, the fire gave way to the candle, which gave way to the kerosene lantern, which gave way to the incandescent electric light bulb, and on to the LCD lighting unit. This stage marks a return to the beginning and stage 1 (identify and define the focus problem).

In actual implementation a wise teacher would offer a class of students a challenge that is broad-based enough to allow all students, whether working as individuals or preferably, as teams, the opportunity to select their own specific focus problem, yet narrow enough so that they all have the sense of working in the same realm of inquiry and on a similar effort or project. For instance, the challenge might be for students to select an aspect of a city that people find difficult and that detracts from the quality of life, and then come up with a solution to make it better. Or perhaps they might be challenged to come up with a food item that would be more appealing or practical than those available currently, or to come up with a way to make the average house or apartment more livable.

Little BIG Idea

Age is no barrier to students becoming innovators. For a number of years the Australian power company, Origin Energy, has run a national competition titled "Origin's littleBIGidea, the big competition for inventive kids." This event, for students in grades three through eight who develop and share their highly innovative ideas, rewards a group of winners with a trip to Florida and a visit to NASA. Online, the program describes itself as providing a platform for students to continue Australia's rich tradition of innovation. The solar hot water, the black box flight recorder, the fridge, and the bionic ear, amongst others, were invented and developed in Australia. The top 12 ideas—including the three overall winners—are selected based on an exceptional demonstration of originality, creativity, practicality, imagination, and innovation.

This program reaches out to teachers by encouraging and supporting them to make it part of what they do in the classroom. Its web resource for teachers (**littlebigidea.com.au**) states: "This is a unique opportunity for kids to learn about idea generation and creative problem solving with a practical focus. It's a broad, open brief, which means all students can participate equally, regardless of whether they're into science and technology, design, humanities or the arts."

The program is simple in structure. Students are directed to come up with a great idea and describe it in words plus a video or image. According to the website, "There are no limits on how big your idea is. It could be a new invention, an improvement to something that already exists or a clever idea that helps make the world around us a better place…Every idea is welcome. No idea is too little or too big. The important thing is how it can help people or make their lives easier. We're looking for original ideas, but we understand this isn't always as simple as it sounds. If you find your idea already exists in some shape or form, try thinking about a fresh new take on it—could your idea be a new and improved version, for example? If you had unlimited money and lots of help, it should theoretically be possible to make your invention or bring your idea to life." (Origin Energy Limited, 2015).

What results are some intriguing entries, many of which can be described as well thought out elevator pitches accompanied by illustrations, demonstrations, and explanations. Here's a small sampling of student entries that were prepared, submitted, reviewed, and appreciated by the public in the convenient form of YouTube videos:

- **Height-adjustable wheelchair** (youtube/pYIxXq4kmjg)

- **Switching off and buying renewable energy** (youtu.be/NIa3y-pmjCw)

- **Recycling water** (youtu.be/SsUn6eLVq64)

- **Locating microchip** (youtu.be/0JqrcUOvhUQ)

In implementing such challenges and in following an innovation framework like the one shared here, students might be broken up into innovation teams, given a period or two for each stage of the process to discuss, reflect, identify, and describe a focus problem of their choice (that relates sufficiently to the challenge given by the teacher); to research; to generate a list of solutions; to select and develop a solution; and finally to apply and share their solution.

There is some clear and strong crossover here with project-based learning, in which students must clarify and communicate their idea, prepare a product and bring it to life (this might take the form of a slideshow-style digital presentation, an uploaded video, an interactive digital poster, and so forth), and ultimately present it to an audience.

Teaching Problem Solving

Problem solving in some contexts can be seen as open-ended and thus a function of creativity. For instance, in finding a solution to the problem of a horse's failing health, a veterinarian may explore a variety of factors and solutions: diet, exercise, environment, infection, and so on. As a result, numerous solutions may be arrived at. In the context of school, though, we often see problem solving as necessarily involving a single, "correct" path to explore, resulting in a single solution. It is the approach and process used in determining the solution that involves creativity.

Math class word problems are a prime example of this. Traditionally, such word problems are presented in classes where the focus is not on developing creativity. Indeed, the approach to teaching word problems has often been to have students see such problems as falling into patterns and then to select from a previously learned vocabulary of computational skills for appropriate ones to "plug in" to the word problem in order to solve it. This sort of thinking does fall into the realm of creative thinking, but not in especially deep and meaningful ways. Further, if one is to reflexively reach for solutions from a pre-set, pre-learned repertoire, there is no motivation for, or understanding of, the necessity of, creating new ones on the fly as they are needed. In other words the shallow type of thinking about problem solving we need to move past is what today's variety of word problem instruction further inculcates.

It should be noted that there is a sector within the mathematics education community that sees its mission strongly as promoting and informing math instruction to be a prime agent of fostering creativity. For example, the University of Cambridge's NRICH Enriching Mathematics website shared an article titled "Developing a Classroom Culture That Supports a Problem-solving Approach to Mathematics" (nrich.maths.org/10341) that offers "practical ways to investigate aspects of your classroom culture. It also offers suggestions to help you develop the culture further so that students are encouraged to develop as independent mathematicians with strong problem-solving skills (Pennant, 2013)."

There are a number of concepts and approaches from the development and application of open-ended creativity that can be applied to developing problem-solving skills. Beginning by, a) defining and clearly stating the problem is one important element. While, in the end, one's efforts may narrow down to selecting just one approach to a single solution, b) brainstorming and listing possible choices can bring clarity to the process and provide impetus to move it forward. Once the approach has been selected, c) careful implementation is necessary, with adjustments made as the implementation is undertaken. Eventually, when a satisfactory solution is selected, refined, and defined, d) its results must be checked and tested to verify that it is indeed correct. If not, rethinking, refining, and subsequent tests and trials must be undertaken. And finally, e) the solution needs to be prepared for presentation so that it can be shared with peers or others who may give feedback on the success of the solution and its appropriateness to the problem tackled. Reflecting on the above stages of solving problems reveals similarities in both the general approach and in the specific steps taken. Above all, reflecting on the process from start to finish, on the approach taken as well as the results obtained, will add a richness of thinking to such activities that goes far beyond simply doing something to get to a correct answer.

There are, of course, variations on the problem-solving frameworks just detailed. In the (free, downloadable) PDF book *Research-Based Strategies for Problem-Solving in Mathematics K-12*, created by the Florida Department of Education, the process is narrowed down to the following four stages:

1. Understanding the problem
2. Devising a plan to solve the problem
3. Implementing the plan
4. Reflecting on the problem

(Florida Department of Education, 2010)

These, in turn, are further developed. For example, Table 4.1 shares the substrategies the book offers for the second stage, which has to do with devising a plan.

Table 4.1: Substrategies for Problem-Solving Strategy 2: Devising a Plan

DEVISING A PLAN TO SOLVE THE PROBLEM			
Hypothesize Estimate Discuss/share Strategies	Guess and check Make an organized list Look for a pattern	Eliminate possibilities Use logical reasoning Draw a picture	Use a formula Work backward Explain the plan

Source: Florida Department of Education

Another good reference for a model in how to teach students problem solving can be found on the website of the University of Waterloo's Centre for Teaching Excellence. Among the rich body of approaches and methods suggested there are the "Principles for teaching problem solving" and "Wood's problem-solving model" (tinyurl.com/z2rq9fs). These can be practically adapted for the classroom.

One essential aspect of teaching problem solving involves modeling of problem-solving attitudes and behaviors. In the thought provoking article "How You Can Help Children Solve Problems" on the Scholastic website, author Ellen Booth Church states: "Think about your own approach to problem solving. Whether you're aware of it or not, children are always watching you. They observe how you deal with problems as examples of ways they might solve problems themselves. Talk about problem solving. When problems arise in the room, discuss your thought processes as you work through the problem ..." (Church, 2012)

It's useful to think of students in this sense as thinking and problem-solving apprentices who can internalize successful strategies and behaviors by observing them in action, which is a very powerful way to learn an essential body of knowledge.

In a heartwarming video titled "Find 3 Ways" posted on the Teaching Channel website (teachingchannel.org/videos/problem-solving-math), third grade teacher, Ms. Saul, explains her successful approach to teaching problem solving in the area of math. The video begins with her asking her class, "Is it okay to make mistakes?" and reassuring them that "we learn from them. Mistakes are easy to fix." She explains that "establishing a strong classroom culture is essential ... we want them to try and try and try again ... we want them to wrestle with a problem and stay with it."

She goes on to explain that in order to accomplish this she uses the Find 3 Ways approach in which she challenges her students to find three possible solutions to a math problem. Interestingly, she explains that in stating the challenge she appeals to the students' sense of empathy so that they feel they are actually helping her solve the problem through their creative thinking. In the word problem she shares with the students she grounds their thinking in real-world situations, in this case helping four teachers figure out how much lunch they can purchase with $20 between them. She begins by discussing the problem, and after the students help her put it in words that all can understand, it is recorded on the board at the front of the classroom. She states for her students that their initial wrestling with the problem is independent work, and she then provides paper-based tools for them to launch into working on it and to organize and record their experimental thinking. "They have four minutes to wrestle with the problem independently and to solve it in as many ways as they can think of." After this segment of the activity, students break up into small groups to discuss the success or failure of their independent thinking and efforts. "It's a chance for them to have discourse over what they're doing." Eventually, students go to the front of the class and share their work and, importantly, explain it. "It's not me dictating how they should get to a particular result … it opens up doors for consulting with one another and collaboration, which are life skills that everybody needs." (Teaching Channel, 2016)

In an inspiring video provided by Education Texas and featuring the high school geometry class of Ms. Mickle (teachingchannel.org/videos/math-problem-solving-strategies), this accomplished teacher talks about the "tools" she teachers her students to use in solving the problems she assigns them. "If you're solving a problem you're going to use properties, you're going to use a definition, you're going to use conjectures, and theorems … process of elimination, and just pure logic … and estimation and substitution. Every problem can be solved by using those tools. If you know the rules of the game, anybody can play!" (Teaching Channel, 2016)

Free Resource for Developing Problem-Solving Skills

This 12-page PDF from Stenhouse titled, *10 Games That Promote Problem-Solving Skills* (stenhouse.com/assets/pdfs/8247ch10.pdf) offers easy-to-implement classroom games that stimulate thinking in the area of problem solving. These can serve as models for further game-based activities that can be part of an overall approach to problem solving that is embraced as part of a classroom's culture and its yearlong efforts. A wide variety of thinking skills are addressed in these 10 examples. These do not require technology to play. However, it isn't difficult to imagine how technology might be tapped to record both the action of these games when played by students and the content they generate in doing so.

INTERVIEW

Michele Haiken

Michele is a middle school literacy educator, blogger, and instructor of graduate school education courses.

MG: How do you integrate creativity into how you teach your students?

MH: I do a project with my students that I call The Product in the Box. I set before my students a box filled with things, recycled objects. The students have to select one and create something with it, or create a new use for it.

I used to teach a career exploration class which had an element of entrepreneurship, and I used this project as a way to begin the course. Now, I do Genius Hour on Fridays and once a month I'll kick start Genius Hour with an activity where I tell the students they must rearrange the things in the box and create things out of what they find inside. The students are able to use all or a few of the materials in the box to create a new product.

They're allowed to use scissors and I allow them a yard of tape, but at the end of the period they have to sell what they have to the rest of the class. What's the connection? You need to be creative to be an entrepreneur.

MG: So the product is an artifact of student creativity. What about the sales pitch the students do for it?

MH: Often, I capture these presentations using the Vine app, and I take a lot of digital photos, too. Vine, allows me to take a 10-second video and post it online. Things that happen in my class that I feel are exciting and relevant to what my class is working on I post to my blog (theteachingfactor.com).

MG: One conceptual issue that comes up for teachers is whether they should teach creativity directly as a specific skill set or focus on and involve student creativity as a way to address other learning goals. How do you see your integration of creativity into your teaching?

MH: I think that I don't teach creativity, per se. I see it more as tapping into student creativity for a variety of purposes. There are moments when I ask the students to stop and reflect and use their metacognition. But in an activity like The Product in the Box, I'm asking students to tap into their creativity for a purpose. They're so used to rote responses and supplying answers for questions in a textbook. So when you say to the students, "I want you to create something," they look at you with disbelief because they're rarely asked to do that sort of thing.

My students definitely take a learning adventure with me when I assign this sort of activity—my classroom can be loud, it can be messy, and sometimes it doesn't look like my kids are learning or doing anything, but by the end, they often produce incredible solutions to the problems I present them with.

MG: How does Genius Hour in your classroom align with student creativity?

MH: My students see Genius Hour as "their time," and they love it. It's their time to pursue what they are interested in. I had a student design her own line of clothing; I had another start her own writing blog. My directions to them are that they should "do something" and it should help the community in some way. And many of them do just that.

Genius Hour is something that comes from the creativity and maker movement that was introduced over a year ago. I jumped on it and it's been very successful in my classroom. I make a commitment to my students that Monday through Thursday we're going to get through the tough, rigorous Common Core–oriented material, and then Friday is theirs to pursue their interests and their passion in learning. I read some material by colleagues that they made their Genius Hour dedicated to benefiting the community, and I went with that idea. My challenge to the students, ever since, has been "Build it, make it, do something . . . but it's got to benefit the community."

PART 2

The
CREATIVE
Learning
Environment

The creative act thrives in an environment of mutual stimulation,
feedback, and constructive criticism in a community of creativity

— William T Brady

Much can be accomplished to foster student creativity simply by establishing an environment in which it is nourished and encouraged. It's also true that without a supportive environment, creativity may simply fail to thrive. What sort of environment will best support students in developing their creativity? What are the needed elements? What can teachers do right away to begin evolving the traditional classroom into a creativity-friendly space?

Part Two of this book shares insights and information in an attempt to answer these questions. Chapter 5 discusses how technology, functions to establish a creativity-friendly environment, identifying types of resources and the sorts of student activity and approaches to creative work they support. These include the fresh ways that today's digital-age learning activities differ from traditional ones, including student collaboration and publishing and dissemination of student work. Chapter 6 discusses the cultural environment established in a creative classroom, the sorts of attitudes and understandings held by creative learners, as well as the behaviors and rituals that take place there as students form a supportive creative community. Chapter 7 looks at the phenomenon of student creativity and the creative process and illustrates a variety of ways that technology facilitates them. Chapter 8 discusses the essential element of assessment as it relates to developing and encouraging student creativity. This is approached by reflecting on and directly referencing a number of the learning standards documents that drive and inform a good deal of school-based instruction, currently. Among these are the ISTE Standards for Students, The Common Core ELA and math standards, the National Core Arts Standards, and Partnership for 21st Century Learning guidelines. Examples of creativity-based student activities as well as rubrics and other approaches to assessing student creative efforts are included as well.

Chapter 5

Collaborative Learning Spaces

Necessary elements for a fertile learning environment—one that fosters the development of creativity and innovation—include the physical aspects of the learning space: lighting, appropriate acoustics, sufficient and suitable workspaces, places to store materials and projects in various stages of development, areas where students may concentrate on their own and others where they can collaborate in small groups, areas to support the sharing of their work, and of course technology resources. Of equal importance is the virtual learning space, offering opportunities for collaboration, sharing, and interaction that extend beyond the walls of a classroom.

Advantages of Technology

Not only can digital resources replace a great many physical items—including visual arts materials (e.g., paints, brushes, modeling clay, and so forth), musical instruments, specialized video and audio equipment, and the like—but technology also provides virtual spaces in which students' projects are easy to store, locate, and retrieve. Such virtual environments allow students' work to be exhibited and viewed with ease, and provide a venue for peer feedback.

This virtual space established by technology can offer invaluable dimensions to a creative learning environment. One very impactful way is through online collaboration, which allows students to get together, share work, and give one another support and feedback without their having to move about to access and work in a group space. Technology can also extend student access to things required for their creative efforts. Visual art projects, for instance, might be accessed at home. This allows the students to put in extra time on their projects, whereas access to a physical art room after the closing of school would be impossible. For that matter, such virtual materials need not require control over their consumption (to conserve supplies), and keeping the materials and the space in which they are used neat and functional is infinitely easier than in the real world.

Collaboration and Digital Resources to Support It

Today's student creators often need to collaborate, and they must have the permission and the means to do so provided by their classroom-management–sensitive teachers. In the world beyond school, projects that depend on creativity are very frequently implemented by teams who create as a focused group. However, re-creating this essential approach represents a very significant organizational shift from the traditional classroom in which whole group instruction and individual study are dominant ways that students work and learn.

True, "group work" is an instructional model with a long track record, although for many teachers it is an approach that proves challenging, both in keeping students on task and managing a classroom in general. This is because students necessarily are given permission to organize and pace their own work (to the degree the teacher stipulates), to move from their assigned seats to their group location, and to talk and communicate as their work dictates. The learning advantages are potentially great, though, especially as we move our learning goals from memorization of facts and applications of basic skills routines to one in which thinking, meaning, and creativity, all with important social learning dimensions, are important goals.

In the Edutopia blog post titled "Deeper Learning: A Collaborative Classroom Is Key," Rebecca Alber gives some sage wisdom about teaching that features student collaboration. She highlights an oft-cited framework, the "Seven Norms of Collaboration" (state.gov/m/a/os/43984.htm), which provides a list of behaviors necessary for members of groups to succeed at their collaboration. Importantly, she also points out that collaboration is one of the 4Cs (communication, collaboration, critical thinking, and creativity), a conceptual framework shared by the Partnership for 21st

Century Learning, an organization that see collaboration and creativity as being closely related and in support of each other (Alber, 2012).

Technology offers a great deal of support to teachers when implementing student collaboration. In fact, it offers many refinements and improvements. For one thing, students in a classroom who have access to computers or tablets may collaborate from their assigned seats by moving into a virtual collaboration space, precluding the need for moving throughout or rearranging the classroom. Another refinement is that while organizing a class of students so that they can move out of traditional, whole class instruction mode and into their work group arrangements can take a good deal of effort and attention on the part of the teacher. Doing this for one project, whereby each student is a member of one group, is likely all that a teacher can manage at any given point in the school year. However, by doing this virtually, online or over a school network, with students' real-world movements not necessary, students can effectively be broken up into any number of different groups, and working on several project simultaneously across the curriculum.

Further, such group work often has to be accomplished during class time when students are physically assembled together. If done virtually, students can easily and conveniently continue their work after designated hours for collaboration, including at home and over the weekend Also, by grouping students in virtual collaborative groups, students may come together for specific projects although they are in different classes or grades, or at school locations that are remotely located from one another.

Some tools and approaches to support virtual collaboration include:

EDMODO

Edmodo (edmodo.com) is an online social media/collaboration platform that allows for the creation of groups in a variety of ways. When teachers requested the ability to create small groups within their larger groups—so students could better collaborate on projects—Edmodo introduced a Small Groups feature.

GOOGLE DRIVE

Google Drive (drive.google.com) is a very popular and easy to use resource for sharing documents, spreadsheets, slide presentations, and so forth. To send a file or folder with someone so that they can view, edit, or comment on it, you can share it with them directly in Google Drive, or through a link or email attachment. Anyone you share the file or folder with will see changes made as they happen so that everyone can be on the same page and you can get feedback quickly.

WEB CONFERENCING

Web conferencing is another approach to supporting and extending the possibilities of collaboration for students. Students may meet online as a small, collaborative group using resources like Skype, Google+, FreeConferenceCall, and Zoom. I've personally used Zoom (zoom.us) for this purpose with good results. As of this writing, it offers a fully functional account free of charge, although sessions are limited to 30 minutes. This sort of resource allows for small groups to see and hear one another using the webcams in their devices, and they can also share text and images. Some tools, like Zoom, offer a high level of security and privacy, and they also offer the ability to record sessions and share them online after the session has completed.

Resources and Tools to Support Student Creative Work

Beyond the single function of collaboration, the creative learning environment will need to provide learners with a variety of resources and tools. Some must have an actual, physical presence, but certainly a very high percentage of them can be digital.

One way of understanding the evolving form and function of the creative learning environment is to think of it as a digital sandbox, an experimental laboratory.

Just a decade or two ago, providing students with a sandbox that was adequate to support their development as creators would have required the dedication of an entire classroom space, a vast array of tools and materials, and the capacity to keep them organized and functional. Storing student projects in various states of completion, too, would have required a great deal of space and organizational resources. Now, however, through the near ubiquity of easy to use and easily available digital resources, a virtual sandbox far richer than any one might have assembled in the real world is within the grasp of teachers who are interested in providing such for their students.

As students create they have need for resources, whether they are working on posters, books or magazines; works of art or music; puppets, displays, and models; machines, contraptions, or devices; or anything that captures their fancy and solves the problems and challenges set before them. With access (at least part of the time) to connected devices, whether they be laptops, tablets, or smartphones, tools for the above things are available and accessible without need for additional space or special environments.

To illustrate, the following are descriptions of the types of digital resources that can serve a community of young creators well.

CAPTURE TECHNOLOGY

Capture technology is a digital resource that proves invaluable in a variety of ways. It provides students with the ability to easily capture images, still or video, as well as audio. If a collage or mashup is the medium a student is working with, then capture technology can greatly facilitate the collection of source material. Capture technology is also highly useful for recording snapshot records of works in progress. This can be a supportive tool in reminding the creator of experiments previously tried and the previous states of a work as it moves toward a possible finish. Capture technology can also be the way of preserving finished products, particularly performances or other forms that don't have a built-in methodology of being recorded. Common resources used for capture technology include digital cameras, including the camera functions of smartphones, flatbed scanners, and digital audio recorders.

PUBLISHING AND SHARING

The final phase of a creative-focused student project is sharing it with an audience. Directing the product or solution to an audience lends it authenticity. For those efforts that can be described as applied creativity, clearly the response of an audience is a natural facet of the work. Further, the resource and format used to share student creative work can shape its final look, feel, and shape. A blog is a good example. A blog is a good publishing resource as it allows for feedback from the audience. While blogs are resources intended to publish text and images, they also take these elements and force them into the format that the blog format requires, sometimes detracting, sometimes adding to content nicely, but always exerting an influence on it.

Before the advent of commonly available classroom technology, publishing and sharing in schools could only take the form of a few samples of student "best work." These samples might, for example, be tacked up on bulletin boards lining the hallway walls or require nervous students to present orally to peers from the front of the classroom or at the edge of the school auditorium stage. Technology has vastly improved the options and reach available to students. Common varieties of sharing resources are blogs and creator-friendly, template-driven websites, online media (YouTube, SchoolTube, SoundCloud, etc.), document sharing resources (Scribd, SlideShare, etc.), and publishing resources for text and media (issuu, bandcamp, iTunes, etc.).

ADDITIONAL RESOURCES

Teachers will likely need to provide access to a great many other varieties of resources and tools, as well. A partial list might include:

- Creative thinking and composing tools (word processing, visual art, music, digital video and audio, animation)

- Game authoring programs

- Curation tools

- Journaling/portfolio apps

- Storytelling tools and websites

- Presentation, and multimedia mashup tools

Fortunately, there is an abundance of these resources. Many of them are free, and classroom tested and proven. See Part Four of this book for a more comprehensive listing of tools and resources.

It is worth mentioning that effective use of these technologies requires that students be provided access to a sufficient amount of time to be productive (and nonproductive as required for creation), to experiment, to share, and to reflect. This time must be planned for by the teacher who is interested in developing student creativity. See the section on the genius hour in Chapter 9 for some discussion of this.

INTERVIEW

Jamie Kaspar

Jamie is a music educator and one of the leaders of of the ISTE Arts & Technology Professional Learning Network.

MG: You're an arts instructor, a music teacher. What should teachers, both arts teachers and other subject area teachers, understand about student creativity?

JK: Learning in the arts does not necessarily foster student creativity. Teachers have to structure learning in ways that require students to generate and evaluate ideas. Luckily, many of the traditions we have in all five arts disciplines—dance, media, music, theater, and visual arts—do this. Dance educators often refer to their practice as "solving movement problems." Media artists, including those in film, have to make technology work in a way that manifests their ideas. Musicians, especially live creators like DJs and loopers, must engage in a nearly

instantaneous process of idea generation, evaluation, and refinement. Such musicians model for a great number of students how they can take the freedom to create original music following their inspiration and ideas, even if they haven't put time and effort into learning traditional, formal music approaches and structures.

Live looping is the recording and playback of a piece of music in real time, using either dedicated hardware devices called loopers or looping software running on a computer. A good example of a looper whose work I admire is Mike Yanchak, a Pittsburgh-based vocal percussionist and live looper. His website (onemouthmusic.com) and the videos featured there illustrate the process of looping and the sorts of creative music products that can be created through using it.

MG: When we talk about student creativity and the things that teachers can do to put students in touch with it and develop it, what are we talking about?

JK: Most creativity researchers use originality and appropriateness of ideas as two indicators of creativity. This means that students need to practice generating original ideas and gauging them for usefulness. In general music, this might look like composing short soundtracks to everyday events, then presenting them to other classes for comment and feedback. In performing ensembles, this could mean allowing students to group themselves into small ensembles and find or modify and perform a piece of music using those instruments or voices.

MG: How about resources? Which resource would you most recommend to teachers trying to understand student creativity through the lens of music instruction? Something that a broad spectrum of teachers could adopt and put to good use?

JK: My favorite resource is the website Music Creativity Through Technology (musiccreativity.org). The authors have provided a list of resources to help teachers reach students who choose not to engage in performing ensembles. Their ideas focus on fostering student creativity through technology.

MG: Any special recommendations for teachers who are looking for a high-value resource or resources to develop student creativity?

JK: Another great resource that can be found in most communities is artists who engage in live creation. If you can find someone who is a live looper, DJ, or similar performer, it is worth your time to sit with that person and ask questions. With new apps like Loopy (loopyapp.com), students can practice the basics of live looping with minimal equipment costs.

Chapter 6

The Cultural Environment

It may be that the cultural environment established to support the development of student creativity is even more important than the resources put at the disposal of students for this purpose.

By making a manageable number of essential changes to the way students understand the classroom community's role in their learning and the development of their creative capacities, a fertile and favorable climate can be established. This chapter presents the specific cultural and functional characteristics of a classroom developed to foster and support student creativity. Among these are the shared beliefs and attitudes that will be supportive; the types of practices, behaviors, and rituals commonly found in such environments; and the physical and functional elements needed for students to share their creative efforts, expand their abilities, and collaborate and function as a community of learners focused on the mutual development and appreciation of creativity.

Ground of Being

Above all, the creativity-focused learning environment needs to identify itself as such. Doing so lets outsiders know that one dimension of the most core work

undertaken there is the development of creativity, and also reminds and reinforces this for members of the class community that occupy it. This may be accomplished by signage or statements announcing this in websites and online spaces maintained for the class community. It may be accomplished by the conspicuous presence of functional elements, like display cases, screening areas, and hard copy libraries of creative products done there. Certainly, such a classroom or class learning environment would do well to put out its own newsletter, journal, website, or digital news publication as an extension of the physical space it occupies. However it is communicated, it is essential that the community occupying the space identifies itself as one that is interested in, honors, and is committed to the creative act and in developing its creative capacities.

A "Safe" Space

The safety of those working in the creativity-focused environment is paramount. Bedrock expectations must include the understanding that all who work there will be respected for their efforts, no matter how successful, and that such respect will be mutually afforded to one another. It must be established that all participants may take whatever sort of risk is needed to further the processes of their creative efforts, and trust that the community and its individual citizens will support one another in them.

Supportive Assumptions, Understandings, and Habits of Mind

The following are beliefs and behaviors and the conditions to support them. They will go a long way toward establishing learning environments that foster the development of creativity in those who work within them:

Students need time to be creative. While accountability for student time is fine, students need to have some time allocated for investigation, experimentation, seeking and reflecting on feedback, revisions, and imagining. Students in an environment that makes developing their creativity an important goal will have a relationship to time that is somewhat different than in environments in which this is not the case.

There is no single right answer. Far better than to deduce the sole correct answer that a test question demands is generating a variety of possible responses among which to choose. This will result in increasingly creative individuals who continually generate more sophisticated and imaginative solutions to problems.

Mistakes are good; it's important to make them. If understood and interpreted properly, mistakes can be viewed as signposts on the path to eventual success.

Mistakes are opportunities to get it right, lenses through which creative individuals find vital information.

Challenges, not assignments. Is a learning activity an opportunity for students to comply with demands simply to retrieve information and present it to the teacher, or is it an opportunity for the student to think and reflect, and to interpret and generate something personal and original?

Creativity is a social phenomenon. A learning environment that effectively fosters the development of creativity involves interactions and transactions between students. Students "pitch" their ideas to one another and give feedback on them. The creative learning environment must allow and encourage this.

Creativity is a habit. Students work creatively often and consistently, engage in creative rituals, keep portfolios and journals that document and support their creative efforts.

Reflection is an important part of the process of developing creativity. Being reflective about one's creative process supports the development of creative capacities.

Exhibit, Celebrate, and Grow

An important dimension of implementing activities that are calculated to develop student creativity is that they include time and focus to acknowledging the creativity that emerges. This may include time and effort directed at reviewing, analyzing, and appreciating creative student work through focused discussion, sharing of opinions and feedback between peer creators, and perhaps writing about it (both the process of creation and reactions to completed works) in reflective journals and blogs. Exhibits, both real world and virtual, are essential. Creativity is something to be celebrated. This celebration does not just acknowledge that students have been creative but recognizes the learning and personal and intellectual growth that accompanies it.

Resources

To gain a deeper understanding of the cultural environment surrounding creativity, a few resources in particular are worth reviewing:

Josh Bolkan's THE Journal article, "Harvard Graduate School of Ed Debuts Free Online Library of Student Work" (tinyurl.com/zot6gxx)

From the Mind/Shift blog: "Can Any School Foster Pure Creativity?" (tinyurl.com/hxbrv8v) and "Growth Mindset: How to Normalize Mistake Making and Struggle in Class" (tinyurl.com/qaojk4a).

INTERVIEW

Tim Needles

Tim is a visual arts teacher and a popular blogger. Tim has taught visual arts and media arts for close to two decades. His blog, Art Room 161 (artroom161.blogspot.com), is updated daily and often incorporates uploaded images from his classes.

MG: People often assume that art class is all about creativity—that it automatically makes students creative. How does this square with your experience as an art teacher?

TN: Creativity is at the center of what I do. When I was in school, art class was often formulaic, and everyone created the same thing and ended up with the same art at the end. That may be fine for teaching technical skill. Now, for me, as an artist, I see creativity as a vital part of art, and so I use a couple of different approaches to get kids thinking creatively. You need to get out of the box of the physical classroom at times. I often experiment and try to find things to try to push the creativity. It's a funny thing to try to get a room full of 30 students to be creative at the same time. It takes some work to get there.

And this is not the mindset that I find is true for many of my fellow teachers. There certainly are teachers of other disciplines in my school and district who see the kinds of things we do in my class and respond to them positively, and I like to collaborate with them. But teaching creativity is not the norm. Even in my art department, there are teachers who are rather traditional. For example, in their classes everyone might be doing the same still life.While there may be a use for that, but I think you could teach that same skill set and get students to be creative at the same time. I try to find ways to have the students push their own expectations and come up with original ideas.

MG: How have you made creativity a prime focus of your art classes?

TN: When I came into the school, the idea was to teach the students the skills and vocabulary of art and then teach creativity in the advanced classes. But after a few years I realized that wasn't enough. To me, creativity is like a muscle

that you need to use—the more you use it, the better you get—and it should be presented early and built up. I find that a lot of students really don't understand what creativity is; they have some misconceptions. Often you hear "I'm not creative" or "I can't be creative" from students and need to fight that thinking.

I think a good teacher has a nourishing atmosphere in their classroom that allows students to be creative. Skills can be taught to anyone, but with creativity . . . you need a degree of personal drive and work to understand it because it's not the same thing for everyone. For some it comes naturally. For others it's a little more of a challenge, and you have to tweak the things you do in the classroom to support them.

First and foremost, I try to model creativity. That helps to get students on board. As an artist I share some of what I do. When I use technology, I use apps like Vine and YouTube to show some of the process behind the work. It goes a long way in setting the stage to get people more interested. With some of the students, I don't necessarily let them know that I'm trying to get them to be creative.

———————————————————

MG: What sorts of activities and challenges do you like to present to your students to nourish and grow their creativity?

TN: In my class we often do animation. As a teacher I understand that giving challenges and establishing limitations in the assignments helps push creativity. I find that "putting students in a box" helps nourish creativity. The students don't necessarily understand that that's why I add those elements. They understand the challenge, but not necessarily the creative aspect of it. Limitations really do help you be creative as an artist. Often I'll have them do a short animation, and maybe I'll require them to add some animals, or maybe a letter of the alphabet. I change it up as I go, because as a teacher you have to stay fresh, too. I don't want to do the same thing over and over again. Adding the limitations pushes the students' creativity, and they may not be aware of that until the end when we talk about the work and the results they produced. Ultimately, it's important they know that they were creative and that we celebrate it.

Having freedom makes being creative even harder than having limitations. It's actually more of a challenge to have a lot of freedom. When I teach my AP or advanced students, I let them create their own assignments. They have a lot of freedom, and they can have a lot of trouble with that. Students aren't used to it. It may seem like a good idea at first, but it can really be hard on them.

MG: How do you see your own creative life intersecting with your students developing their own creativity?

TN: There are a couple of elements that go hand in hand with creativity. As a teacher I share some personal things with my students. I follow my bliss. I follow my curiosity about things. I also show the challenges that come with being curious and creative, including failures. One of the challenges with creativity is failure and your reactions to it—how to learn from it and not let it stop you. I keep a sketchbook with me all the time. And I'm always drawing and sketching and making little animations. I share this with my students by using social media, something that has changed my teaching significantly.

I document the creative things I do and use them as teachable moments. So when students are in the middle of a real dilemma and they don't know where to go or what to do next, I will show examples from my own and other artists' work as a way of showing "This is what I did and what another artist did in a similar situation . . . and here's how we dealt with it."

After I get to know my students, I assign them to research and discover specific artists based on what I feel are their needs as learners. Artists who I feel relate to the sorts of things they are interested in and are doing. This makes it interesting for me, too, because I get to learn more about more artists as I and my students look at them and learn about their process together. One of the fortunate things that happens is if, in this context and for this reason, a student studies a contemporary artist, I'll encourage them to contact the artist through social media so we can ask our own questions.

MG: But do you have to be an artist to foster student creativity? Can teachers who don't ordinarily consider themselves creative succeed with this?

TN: I really don't think you need to be an artist to make creativity part of what you do as a teacher. I think one of the big things that art teachers can offer colleagues is not just making creativity part of teaching, but tying creativity together with student engagement, as well as embracing visuals and things that are a bit out of the norm, and giving people permission to fail at things if what they are trying doesn't work at first. Creativity is not a clear-cut thing—it's somewhat difficult to define. You can't understand a student's creativity by looking at tests. It can be hard to quantify. You need to take something of a risk to try to introduce it into your classroom, if you are a somewhat traditional teacher. When we model our success in creative activities, that can help inform and

encourage colleagues. I make myself available to colleagues, and I do that sometimes through social media. Sometimes I work with teachers and students from other disciplines and include them in special art projects I do—not only do the students benefit, but their teachers become more open to the possibility of making creativity part of their teaching.

MG: What are some examples of activities to develop student creativity?

TN: Doodle Dare—Begin with an unfinished drawing, usually an ambiguous one with a character in it, and everyone in the class finishes the drawing. It's a quick lesson. . . . This illustrates creativity, as students can see the differences between their solutions to the challenge, and ponder how it is that they came up with their own personal idea and why it's not the same for all. This approach can be adapted for other subjects as well, such as in writing.

Animation challenges—I give students generally 5 days to complete an animation challenge. I have them use Post-it notes and incorporate live action with the drawings. The project involves the use of Instagram, Twitter, and Vine. In the past, before there was much technology available for teachers, I'd teach animation and it might take several weeks before we actually got to do and see an animation. Now, with these apps, we are animating and seeing results the very first week of a project.

I like quick and spontaneous tools. We create a Twitter hashtag and all of us post our work there so that we can review and compare work anytime. On my Twitter page (twitter.com/timneedles), I list the apps that I like to use for each class. Nothing like free apps for students!

Chapter 7

Student Creativity and Technology

Moving into a teaching practice that embraces the development of student creativity as a focus is a goal that has likely been worthy and relevant for decades. With the advent of near ubiquitous, user friendly digital technologies that can support all manner of intellectual effort, this goal is both a necessity and something that is more achievable than ever before. With technology comes the element of continually accelerating change, a condition for which preparing students implies developing their ability to create solutions and responses to problems, needs, and situations that arise continually. Further, the same technologies that have contributed to this newly heightened learning need are the tools and resources with which effective responses can be created.

This chapter presents some key understandings about how these things may be addressed in the classroom. It examines the specific ways that technology can be applied to student creative work and how technology functions within the context of the types of activities closely associated with such activities and projects. Further, the chapter discusses connections between technology and the sorts of activities found more and more in the evolving intellectual workplace, an environment in which deep thinking, research, and the production and sharing of creative products are becoming essential.

In the article titled "How Can Technology Enhance Student Creativity?" author Saomya Saxena states emphatically:

> Neuroscience research has proved the fact that all children are born with innate creative powers and as they grow up some of them keep their creativity active while others unconsciously keep it dormant. Hence, all of us from being a child have the potential for great, revolutionary creativity and all we need is to realize this potential. (Saxena, 2013)

In another article, this one appearing in Forbes magazine, titled "The 10 Skills Employers Most Want In 20-Something Employees," Susan Adams reported that "the National Association of Colleges and Employers (NACE), a Bethlehem, Pa. non-profit group that links college career placement offices with employers, ran a survey from early August to mid-September where it asked hiring managers what skills they prioritize when they hire college grads ... employers seek basic teamwork, problem-solving, and the ability to plan and prioritize" (Adams, 2013).

Here are the 10 skills employers say they seek, in order of importance:

1. Ability to work in a team
2. Ability to make decisions and solve problems
3. Ability to plan, organize, and prioritize work
4. Ability to communicate verbally with people inside and outside an organization
5. Ability to obtain and process information
6. Ability to analyze quantitative data
7. Technical knowledge related to the job
8. Proficiency with computer software
9. Ability to create and/or edit written reports
10. Ability to sell and influence others

Most of these skills either relate directly to the development of student creativity—including problem solving and innovation—or they strongly relate to skills involved in the act of creation and work on creative projects (Adams, 2013).

Another article, this one from the IBM website, titled "IBM 2010 Global CEO Study: Creativity Selected as Most Crucial Factor for Future Success," states:

> According to a major new IBM survey of more than 1,500 Chief Executive Officers from 60 countries and 33 industries worldwide, chief executives believe that—more than rigor,

management discipline, integrity or even vision—successfully navigating an increasing complex world will require creativity. (IBM, 2010)

An online search will reveal many similar findings reported in a never-ending stream of such articles. At the very least, these often-heard assertions represent something that today's educators should ponder as they continue on their planning and preparation for the educational experience they provide their students. The message is clear, though, and now that we have determined that the development of student creativity is a crucial next step in the evolution of the instructional program provided by our schools, the specifics of how to address this need will have to be carefully considered.

As I mentioned, I began my career as a public school visual art teacher. After many years of involvement with that subject and a strong interest in the integration of visual art across the curriculum, I gradually became more and more involved in the field of instructional technology. This has afforded me a focused understanding of how the area of student creativity and the area of technology support teaching and learning intersect.

Many teachers never really consider the dynamics of teaching art, and they often assume that it is "easy to teach" because it is "fun." It has been my experience that such opinions are based on unfounded, untested assumptions, assumptions that are incorrect. It is not true that all students necessarily love to make art. Many simply are not interested in art activities, although they may find a little uncommitted dabbling to be amusing. Learning to make art, to focus on craft, message, and meaning is a serious undertaking that requires focus, effort, and the ability to press through frustration and difficulty. Simply understanding the works of great artists, alone, can take a good deal of head scratching and brain stretching. Creating original works can be infinitely more difficult. It may superficially appear that "playing" with poster paint is just that, play. But the truth is a skillful teacher must coax and coach students through the complex processes involved in making meaningful, communicative, expressive works of art.

In the context of an arts course, for instance, when working with students who have been assigned an appropriate and worthwhile learning challenge, one can easily observe students who experience frustration. They may find that when they are expected to deal with producing a response or attempting a solution to an open ended challenge, one for which there is no clear right answer, but one for which a unique, personal response, one that will be measured against defined criteria, is frustrating. Effective learning challenges, by the way, are very often those intended

to push the envelope of student understanding and ability. In other words they are designed to provoke a student response that requires a bit of a stretch, intellectually and otherwise.

Further, one easily observes significant frustration with the craft portion of the challenge, the need to draw or sculpt an acceptable visual representation of something, for instance, or perhaps to write a clear and insightful description of something. The irony is that in order to respond to the assigned challenge, the student must have at hand a sufficient level of competency of the craft to be employed in creating the required product or performance. It is common for students to give up before they even begin to try if they sense that the undeveloped level of their skills will result in embarrassing failure. The effect of this is multiplied and complicated when students realize that after working on their product or performance for a considerable period of time, they are disappointed with their own work. After the expenditure of much time and effort, they might be facing certain failure even if they apply more time and effort to the project. And yet more time and energy must be expended should they decide to start over to successfully complete an assignment.

We are talking about months or years invested in developing the skills of representational drawing, learning the notes and scales and chords and theory required to play an instrument, learning the grammar and punctuation and voice rules and conventions to write effectively, and on and on. This is the truth of engaging in the arts, and the sciences, too, if one considers how mathematics and rules of mechanics, electronics, and engineering often dictate even entry level participation in them. Small wonder that experienced art teachers and others attempting to foster creativity in students have to develop a portfolio of approaches. Needless to say, striking a balance can involve offering students experiences of lesser worth. No doubt any subject that involves hard-to-acquire craft/skills, discipline, and sophisticated self-management requires similar considerations.

However, we live in a remarkable age in which technology has transformed the experience of being creative. Technology can empower students to produce sophisticated, highly appealing, professional looking products without the need for talent, for difficult-to-acquire skills, and without great effort. Graphics, artistic images, word processed and desktop published texts, videos, animations, voice and musical recordings, and more are now commonly produced by students of all ability levels, even young ones.

However, when one looks at the works of visual artists like M. C. Escher, Norman Rockwell, or Andrew Wyeth; at the photos of Edward Weston; the comic strips of Charles Schulz or the graphic novels of Neil Gaiman; listens to the music of Marvin Hamlisch; the voice recordings of actors and orators; and on and on, what comes across is that the craft, as well as the product the craft has been employed to produce, are vehicles for something else, something more. I am referring to the message, the statement, the body of ideas communicated. True, the craft and the product may be part and parcel of this, but they are only that: an essential element.

Following this logic we can see how the emergence of technology, a body of resources that provides for the user the skill and craft needed, and its remarkable level of ease and certainty, has liberated the technology user from the effort to develop these skills. The technology user is free to concentrate on the message and meaning, the creativity for which the entire enterprise is directed.

10 Ways Technology Supports and Fosters the Development of Student Creativity

1. **Saving unlimited versions and drafts.** One of the ways that technology supports creativity is by allowing for multiple, no-risk trials and versions of experiments. In the past, each draft or early version of an original product or solution was precious. Once an attempt that altered the piece was taken, the creator would have found it very difficult to return to the earlier version if the new stage turned out to be a path that didn't lead to the desired final result. With technology, work can be saved at every stage, allowing for endless trials and stages. This permits the creator to try different things without risk of losing his or her work and momentum.

2. **Randomizing and presenting quick prompts and associations.** With so much material available on the web and so many ways to retrieve and organize it, generating prompts and suggestions of ideas is far easier than before. Using a search engine, for instance, a creator can enter a single random or focused search word and generate countless unanticipated responses, pairings, and associations with other ideas.

3. **Stimulating creativity through technology's capabilities and characteristics.** In many cases, simply working and interacting with a technology tool can suggest creative directions to take or innovative possibilities previously not imagined. Tech tools work quickly and tirelessly and often lend their own flavor to content, organizing, formatting, and giving style to work just started or in progress.

4. **Organizing and facilitating the creative processes through the use of graphic organizers, flow charts, and related digital resources.** Found in abundance as features of common digital resources like word processors (e.g., MS Word) and/or as (often) free and readily accessible online, a wide variety of information organizing tools are available to users (e.g., alphabetizing, frequency sorting, numbering and hierarchy creating, and so on). As well, visual representational organizing tools (e.g., flow charts, semantic maps, organizational charts, tree hierarchies, and more) can truly empower creators.

5. **Producing satisfying, professional looking products quickly and easily.** Many tech tools produce products that require little hard-earned "craft knowledge" to generate (e.g., word processing/desktop publishing, slide presentations, photo albums, comic strips, animations and animated avatars, and so on). These tools encourage and provide momentum for creators, and help them visualize the evolving shape and impact of their work and see previously unimagined possibilities.

6. **Facilitating collaboration.** One of the core functions of technology is that of facilitating communication between people. Today's tech tools make communication easier and possible in ways previously not imagined (e.g., Skype video calls), and help organize it by creating virtual spaces in which groups can meet privately and exchange information in numerous formats in ways not previously possible.

7. **Providing opportunities for sharing.** One of the reasons to create products and solutions is to present it, ultimately, to an audience (or a group of users in the case of a functional item). Our new, technology-fueled world makes this possible in a great many effective ways. These include formatting original work in ways to generate professional-appearing products; posting text, images, and audio in virtual public spaces (e.g., blogs); open libraries (e.g., YouTube); and allowing for the creation of emailing lists, RSS, and Twitter feeds, and so forth. Using technology, presenting work to an audience is easy, effective, and becomes a well-integrated part of the continuum of steps that make up the end-to-end flow of a creative project.

8. **Allowing for instantaneous feedback.** In many instances technology resources include functions that allow an audience to respond to what's been presented to them (e.g., comments functions of blogs and media sharing resources like YouTube). An audience may also respond to online content by taking advantage of "contact" functions and information (e.g., email addresses) provided by content posters. Social media takes this function of technology a step further by sharing the actual content and resulting feedback with a focused audience.

9. **Supporting the capture and archiving of drafts, versions, presentations of a product, and performances, as well as the retrieval of each.** In many ways, the ability to capture an element to add to a project/product (e.g., image, sound bite, passage of text, and

the like) empowers the creator and expands the possibilities of both the creative process and product. Many items are easily accessible and freely available that make this so (e.g., smartphone stills and video cameras, snip and screen capture software, OS functions of computers and tablets, digital audio recorders, and so on). Once captured, today's devices make storing the material easy. Organizing and retrieving them from digital storage is easily accomplished with a variety of search functions.

10. **Enabling ongoing, process-oriented creativity.** Technology supports process oriented creativity, a variety of approach that involves a series of phases that may culminate in both a finished product and in a subsequent cycle of work to produce ongoing, next generation products or solutions. Consequently, a broad range of technology connections to creative work, which, beyond the advantages they present on their own, contribute to a cycle of next step creative planning and work. These include:

   - production of multiple versions of outlines, storyboards, trials, and drafts;

   - collection of feedback on drafts;

   - collaboration with co-creators;

   - research into what's been created before;

   - the presentation of the finished work to an audience or user group and the collection and analysis of their feedback;

   - based on the above, initial steps in the subsequent cycle of phases of the next generation of creative work or project.

In the Forbes magazine tech blog post titled "How Technology Enhances Creativity," author Greg Satell states: "Technology enhances creativity, it drastically reduces the cost of actualizing our intent. We can search domains, mix and match ideas and test concepts almost effortlessly. That means we can try out a lot more possibilities and increase the chance of producing something truly outstanding" (Statell, 2014).

Students today can produce comic strips that rival in skill and craft (as shown in Figure 7.1) of a professional by using easy-to-acquire (and often free), very user-friendly resources like Pixton (pixton.com), ToonDoo (toondoo.com), and many others that are found easily online. Using a resource like buncee (buncee.com), students can create a new format of creative product, one we might call "digital poster," that mixes images, graphic elements, and text in ways that rival fine examples of classic poster art. These works can also feature sound and animation, resulting in products that even the most accomplished poster artists of the 19th and 20th centuries could never have imagined.

Figure 7.1: Students can explore their creativity and storytelling capabilities through cartoon creation tools such as Pixton.com

Can Technology Be Anti-Creative?

In his probing article in *Educational Leadership* titled "Power Up! Technology and the Illusion of Creativity", Doug Johnson raises some useful questions. First he ponders, "When technology enables a person to make something that looks professional without having to master any degree of craft, does that increase or decrease the likelihood of creativity?" (Johnson, 2014)

This is a good question, but unless we take the position that the craft aspect of a work of art, or any original creation for that matter, is the end and not the means to that end, then the answer to this is a resounding "No!" If we take a look at the art of photography, for instance, we can see a good example of image making that requires little physical training. In fact, the image in every way is made by a machine. It is the photographer's job, though, to select subject, to select the angle and size at which the camera captures the subject and its background, to determine if the lighting is suitable, and so on. Operating the camera requires little beyond pushing a button. In earlier days, camera technology required photographers to adjust aperture and exposure and depth of field. Today, it is most common for cameras to do those things automatically, and countless fine art photographs have been taken with such cameras. That photographers produce a compelling image with modern cameras without struggle does not sacrifice nor negate the creativity involved and expressed through photography.

Johnson further ponders, "And can educators be lulled into a false impression that they have been developing creativity in students when using technologies that produce brilliant-looking results?" Another very useful question, as it brings us back to the appropriate starting point query of asking ourselves, "What is creativity?" The answer is that creativity is not the product or performance, it is the skill set and act of bringing something new and original into the world that is at the heart of what is creative. And, of course, it goes further than that because for us to notice something new and appreciate its impact, it must be meaningful, significant, and offer value. Following the example of a "word cloud" produced using Wordle (wordle. net), a creativity tool that has garnered tremendous attention with teachers because it is free, very easily accessed, and very easy to use, and because it relates to literacy skills, the most core of all curriculum focused on by schools, we can see two possibilities of what students may produce with it: a) an impressive looking but meaningless product, or b) a product that on examination communicates understandings, meaning, insight, and a bit of sparkle. It isn't the craft performed by the resource or the user of the resource that makes the difference between the two; it's the thinking, resourcefulness, and innovative expression carried by the craft.

The overarching point in all of this, however, is that through the use of technology students are freed from the labor, frustration, and limitations of craft so that they can effectively concentrate on the other aspects of creativity, the ones that count most and that we teachers must address.

How Technology Supports Creativity and Creators

Beyond the issue of craft, there are other ways that technology supports, assists, and empowers students in the area of creativity. Here are a few of them:

DEEP SUPPORT FOR THINKING

Technology is available to provide support in the crucial area of thinking that accompanies and drives creativity. Numerous varieties of thinking are involved and can be drawn on in the creative process, among them brainstorming, role playing, associating, randomizing, and so on.

RESEARCH

If one is to create something new, it is essential to know if it has not been done before. Even more essential, perhaps, is to know who else has worked on the idea and what angles others have taken to explore it and what sorts of products have already been produced in response. It is also necessary to find materials with which to shape and flesh out creative ideas. Research is a practical and effective way to address these concerns. Certainly, simple searches, like the use of search engines, is an important part of this research. However, there are other approaches and resources that support creativity. Among these are Google Alerts (google.com/alerts), emailed notices of freshly posted information on subjects identified by the user; and direct collection of information by the researcher, which can be supported by technology, as well, with such tools as Survey Monkey

(surveymonkey.com) to create, disseminate, collate and analyze informational responses, and Evernote (evernote.com) to record, store, and retrieve observations and anecdotal information. All of these resources offer at least a basic level of service free.

COPING WITH THE CREATIVE PROCESS

Discovering that creative ideas and products don't simply come from bolt-from-the-blue Eureka moments of inspiration but can be generated predictably by the use of a variety of processes is both inspiring and empowering. Technology helps the creator use and benefit from the structure of these processes (e.g., the writing process, the design process, and so forth). These processes are especially important in our current era of group and project-based work, a phenomenon borne out in actual practice by some of the most forward thinking and successful companies today, like Apple and Google.

SHARING PRODUCTS AND PERFORMANCES

The element of having an audience to whom to present the results of the creative act elevates the act and process of creativity considerably, particularly within the context of learning. Having an audience lends a sense of importance to creative projects. Understanding that the work will be viewed and evaluated naturally motivates students to produce solutions and products and performances that impress others as being original, significant, and of high quality. Further, in process oriented Creativity, an ongoing sequence of conception, trials or drafts, and then refinements and more advanced versions is empowered and enriched by feedback on what's been created thus far. Audience feedback can be a valuable source of information on how well a draft solution satisfies the challenge it was created to address.

Resources to support students in sharing their creative work with an audience may enhance or frame the work allowing others to see it in its best light, provide a place in which to display or provide access to the audience, and may gather information about the audience, or elicit and relay audience comments about the work back to the student and/or others. This last point may be important as an audience member interested in giving feedback may want to comment on previous comments or take them into consideration when forming his own. All of this can be useful in the ongoing life of a project or creative effort as it works toward its conclusion.

Technology provides a great deal in this regard. There are a variety of web-based resources that may be used for the above purposes:

- Photo /Graphics Sharing Resources. Photo sharing sites like Flickr (flickr.com), Picasa Web Albums (picasaweb.google.com/home), ShutterFly (shutterfly.com), and others allow for users to upload photos and share them with others. Most of these resources allow for a variety of sharing and privacy options. Many of them allow for users to add captions to photos, as well. These sites, while intended for photos will take uploads of any file in common graphics formats like JPG or GIF, allowing students who scan creative work, photograph it, or who convert file formats, to upload such work, as well.

- Audio Sharing Resources: Resources like SoundCloud (soundcloud.com/upload), allow users to upload and share their audio files either by the link or an embeddable "player" they provide. The offer a number of publishing and privacy options. Some, like Clyp It (clyp.it/) allow for audio to be recorded directly on their site from a connected student device and provide a link to the recording for use elsewhere. Others, like Vocaroo (vocaroo.com), allow users to record or upload previously recorded and edited files for sharing.

- Video Sharing Resources: YouTube allows users to upload videos and choose from a variety of options about who can view them. There are numerous alternatives, like TeacherTube (www.teachertube.com) and SchoolTube (www.schooltube.com)

- Text Sharing Resources: Google Drive is a free, easy to use resource that allows users to upload files and choose from a variety of options about who can view, download, or alter it. There are numerous alternatives, like SlideShare (slideshare.net), and issuu (issuu.com)

- Multi-Format Publishing Resources allow for the above to be combined. The perfect example of this for the purpose of sparking and supporting student creative work is the blog. Blogger, for instance, allows students to upload their writing in an attractive and professional-looking online publishing format. Graphics as well as audio, video, and text widgets are easily embedded. The comments feature allows for audience (including the teacher) to respond with text comments, and for other audience members, as well as the poster, to respond to those comments. KidBlog is another blog resource option, among many to choose from (kidblog.org/home.)

See the resource section in Part Four of this book for more options and ideas.

INTERVIEW

Brittany Howell

Brittany is a literacy and family learning specialist with the National Center for Families Learning, the organization that produces and provides Wonderopolis. I invited Brittany to present Wonderopolis alongside the Literacy Professional Learning Network at ISTE's annual conference and interviewed her there. On its website, Wonderopolis describes itself as "Where the Wonders of Learning Never Cease. Explore. Imagine. Laugh. Share. Create. Learn. Smile. Grow."

MG: What is Wonderopolis, and how do teachers use it?

BH: Wonderopolis is a free online resource loved by families, educators, and students alike. Wonderopolis is visited by more than 640,000 users monthly, equaling more than 12 million users since Wonderopolis' inception. The only requirement to use it is that you have internet access.

MG: Can you give me an idea of what teachers find at Wonderopolis?

BH: There is a new Wonder of the Day (an exploration of a curious question) that's uploaded every weekday. In the summer we host Camp Wonderopolis, our free online summer-learning camp. Wonderopolis is about thinking, wondering, and appreciating what an incredible world this is and how much there is to learn and think about. Wonderopolis does that in a format that supports sharing and trading ideas.

MG: What's the Wonderopolis approach to sparking students' imaginative thinking?

BH: We like to say that wonder is all around us, for anyone, at any time. What we love to celebrate at Wonderopolis are those everyday, curious questions that we all have but that we don't ordinarily take the time to explore. That becomes the basis of what we do at Wonderopolis.

MG: That sounds great, but how do you support teachers in making that part of the school day? Teachers are busy, and there are so many things to keep track of. How do you get some of the teachers' bandwidth?

BH: You can sign up to have the Wonder of the Day emailed to you and/or your students. Teachers often make this the basis of some of the work they do with their class. All of the new Wonder questions, by the way, are user generated; the Wonder questions are sent in by the users in response to our invitation to contribute to the Wonder Bank, a body of questions that users have contributed (now well over 34,000). We also acknowledge the person, student or teacher, who sent in the Wonder question.

MG: Beside the Wonder of the Day, what other things will teachers and students find at Wonderopolis to pique their curiosity and wonder and inspire them to think imaginatively and, hopefully, be creative?

BH: One of Wonderopolis' features is a Media Gallery of images and videos—each Wonder features a video and photographic images related to the Wonder question, offering a multimedia approach to the Wonder topic.

MG: While Wonder, Imagination, and Creativity are qualities of thinking, knowing, and learning that are high goals for teachers and students, one favored approach to foster these things within the context of instruction is to align them to the learning of required bodies of knowledge and skills. Does Wonderopolis have things to help in this regard, as well?

BH: The video and images are entertaining and illustrative, so that they are easy to understand. Vocabulary is important in education, and we provide vocabulary and definitions for words that appear in the informational text passage. The Wonder Words are sorted by ability levels and presented in a dynamic way. The words are highlighted in the text provided, and if you hover your cursor over the words, you'll get the definition. Then after you finish, you can take the Wonder Word Challenge, which is a randomized interactive game to check understanding of the vocabulary words. At the end of every Wonder there's a Did You Get It? reading comprehension exercise as well. Each Wonder will also read the words aloud to you and highlight the text as it is read aloud, if you activate that function. This enables readers of all abilities to be more independent of direct teacher support.

Students can practice digital citizenship skills by joining the discussion on each Wonder of the Day and submitting comments to Wonderopolis that express their thinking through their writing—writing that will be seen by others. Each comment then receives a personalized response from Wonderopolis encouraging students to continue wondering and learning.

Chapter 8

Creativity, Assessment, and Standards

If we are to make creativity an important goal and outcome for students in our schools, then it is necessary to consider how to handle the dimensions of assessment and accountability.

In all likelihood, student creativity will not be assessed any time soon in its raw state. In other words creativity as a body of abilities and learned skills will not be assessed on its own in isolation as educators have done in other areas—for instance, in assessing intelligence through the use of tests. Rather, creativity will be taught and measured within the context of existing subject areas. There's little likelihood that a discreet course in creativity, per se, will emerge and gain prominence in our schools' instructional programs. Further, creativity will be seen as a dimension of projects and activities in which numerous dimensions contribute simultaneously to a body of learning outcomes and so will not be taught or assessed in isolation.

Sir Ken Robinson has stated: "The reason I believe you can assess creativity is that creativity is not an abstraction." He goes further, saying:

> To be creative you have to be doing something. It's a very practical thing to be creative. If you were lying in bed all day doing nothing at all nobody would ever accuse you of being creative—unless you did something—unless there's some practical outcome,

eventually. That could be anything. You could be creative in music, in dance, in cuisine, in mathematics, in physical education, in making movies ... anything. It's a practical process of making something .... You can assess creative work providing it's understood that you're looking at particular things, not at broad abstractions .... You can assess student creative work by making it clear that it's being judged as a practical contribution in a particular discipline. (Taken from the YouTube video "Sir Ken Robinson answers your Twitter questions (#askSKR), Question 2: Assessing Creativity")

Few things in our schools stand alone, maintaining a unique and distinctive culture and methodology that isn't part and parcel to the general way of doing and valuing things there. In fact, students, once they are acculturated to the institution of school, often are most comfortable when the implied and explicit rules of the institution in general, are perceived to be in place for the various elements that make up their experience there. Consequently, when implementing instructional activities to develop student creativity, we must consider whether or not to make assessment part of those activities. Since the answer to this question of assessment is most likely to be a "Yes" we must consider how to accomplish it.

Unless we reflect on this we are likely to fall under the sway of a few popular notions about student creativity and teaching to develop it that are counterproductive. One, that it is impossible to measure creativity and two, that the act of assessing creativity strongly discourages it. Both of these concerns, upon careful reflection, appear to be misguided and uninformed.

In a blog post titled "On assessing for creativity: yes you can, and yes you should" Grant Wiggins explains that "it is vital when asking students to perform or produce a product that you are crystal-clear on the purpose of the task, and that you state the purpose (to make clear that the purpose is to cause an intrinsic effect, NOT please the teacher ...), when the student has clarity about the Goal of the task, their Role, the specific Audience, the specific Setting, the Performance particulars, and the Standards and criteria against which they will be judged, they can be far more effective—and creative!—than without such information." (Wiggins, 2012)

Wiggins appears to be describing acts of applied creativity, and shares ideas about dimensions of the task (challenge) assigned to students that represent both support and dimensions of the work by which their performance can be measured. In other words, if the challenge is to produce a brochure to inform or teach about something, we can hold the student accountable for having accomplished that. The rest defines the context within which the challenge is to be addressed and satisfied. For instance, in producing the brochure the student does so from the perspective of a

teacher of an elementary class. Beyond simply teaching, a challenge may call for the goal of the student work to prove something or convince a specific audience about it.

Can we expect students to be creative as they address and satisfy such a challenge? Clearly, if they generate original ideas (original to them), express those ideas originally or uniquely or—and this is very much the way that citizens and information workers of the digital age are, and will continue to be called on to be, creative—if they have put together an original collection of items from a body of sources they've assembled themselves, and put them together in an original manner, then yes, they have been creative. These are things that all students can and should be expected to be able to do and the types of skills and tasks on which their ongoing learning and work beyond school will depend.

Granted, determining "how creative" a product or performance is when compared to the level of creativity represented by another product or performance would be far harder to determine and would likely be far more subjective. Still, by following this simple model and set of criteria, effective assessment and accountability is established. Instructional activities associated with student creativity are therefore: a) students are assigned a challenge in which they must produce a product/performance to address and satisfy a purpose and goal, and to impact the audience to which it is directed, and b) what they produce and present must be original and unique: it must be based on a body of sources and collected items that is original; assembled in a configuration/collection that is original; and assembled and presented in a form that is original.

A rubric may be created and applied to the above instructional scenario to communicate expectations clearly to students, to facilitate the work, and to guide and support the assessment of what the student has produced and achieved. One such rubric appears in the 2013 article titled "Assessing Creativity" by Susan M. Brookhart, who states:

> I created this rubric with some trepidation—because where ther's a rubric, there will be someone who's thinking of using it to grade. Generating a grade is not the intended purpose of the rubric for creativity. Rubrics help clarify criteria for success and show what the continuum of performance looks like, from low to high, from imitative to very creative. For that reason, rubrics are useful for sharing with students what they're aiming for, where they are now, and what they should do next. I do not recommend grading creativity. (Brookhart, 2013)

The rubric, shown in Table 8.1, provides a simple framework on which to analyze and assess student work. It may be used by teachers to inform students of expectations at the outset of a project, by students to guide their own efforts, and by the teacher and the extended community of learners. Its aim is to provide useful, formative information to student creators. It can also be used as a basis for grading, if grading is deemed a need that is part of the overall purpose and function of the instructional experience.

Importantly, this rubric puts emphasis on the processes involved in creative work as well as the products and performances. Along with this comes a dimension of learning of high value, reflection, and self-accountability. As they work toward satis-fying challenge tasks and producing finished products, students should be encour-aged and guided in thinking about and recording what they've done, what worked and what didn't and why, and in explaining why they made the decisions and did the things they did along the way to completing their work. This might take the form of compiling a simple portfolio of work notes and process tools (e.g., simple graphic organizers, check lists, flow charts, and the like) and journaling the ongo-ing, various phases and stages of their work. This not only will help keep students on task and on track, but it will provide evidential material on which both student and teacher can base assessment for the process portion of their work. Moreover, this mirrors actual work and learning practices from the real world of higher educa-tion and the work place.

Through his blog (grantwiggins.wordpress.com) Grant Wiggins provides his own rubric, one that focuses not on the functional, but on the phenomenon of creativity exhib-ited in student work. While teachers can engage students in activities planned to develop their creativity and can provide resources and environments that are sup-portive and conducive to the development of creativity, they cannot "teach" cre-ativity directly in the same sense that a body of fact and simple skills is currently commonly taught in subjects like math in anticipation of the administration of tests as convenient assessments. Wiggins's rubric provides a hierarchy of six levels of assessment for the creativity demonstrated in student work, each of them accompa-nied by four or more defining descriptors to help students and teachers determine which level to ascribe to the work or parts of it. These six levels of assessment are presented in the creativity rubric shown in Table 8.2.

This approach may be useful if the rubric is seen as a formative tool, with the understanding that students will be afforded an ongoing opportunity to develop their creativity through a continuing series of challenges that require creative responses. This would be particularly useful in an environment in which the class-room community has the opportunity to self-analyze and reflect on accomplish-ment and growth of creativity over the course of a project and through an ongoing

Table 8.1: Rubric for assessment and accountability of student performance for instructional activities requiring student creative responses.

AREA OF STUDENT PERFORMANCE ON PROJECT	PERFORMANCE DESCRIPTION **FUNCTIONAL:** Student followed directions and responded and produced to the extent indicated and assigned.		PERFORMANCE DESCRIPTION **EXCELLENT:** Student responded with enthusiasm, originality beyond the level needed to merely satisfy the assignment. The student work shows inspired response, initiative, originality, inspired creativity, etc.
1. Originality and sufficiency of approaches and methods of identifying, locating, selecting, and generating sources and product elements		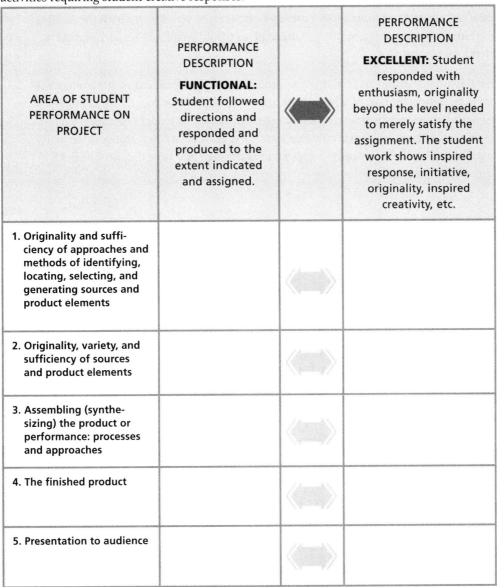	
2. Originality, variety, and sufficiency of sources and product elements			
3. Assembling (synthesizing) the product or performance: processes and approaches			
4. The finished product			
5. Presentation to audience			

Note that this rubric lists the anticipated flow of student creative work, taking into account both process-oriented work (e.g., steps 1 and 2) and product oriented work (e.g., steps 3–5). The performance description relates to work that is deemed passing (or beyond), and the work itself is deemed functional to excellent. The arrow in the column between these descriptions indicates that at teacher discretion, students may be rated incrementally.

series of projects with individual students following this for their own work and that of their classmates. Whole-group discussions in which comparisons are made between a variety of students' responses along with observations about the success of things tried and suggestions for alternatives would establish the sort of culture that fosters creativity.

Establishing a strong and balanced approach to the development of student creativity is an important part of what can be accomplished in the classroom. Elements of both rubrics may be blended so that students at various stages of addressing a creative challenge in a learning project are cued as to what the purpose of an activity is, what is valued in producing work to address it, and how they will be held accountable for their performance.

Table 8.2: Creativity Rubric

6	The work is *unusually creative*	The ideas/materials/methods used are novel, striking, and highly effective.
5	The work is *highly creative*	The ideas/materials/methods used are imaginative and effective.
4	The work is *creative*	The ideas/materials/methods used are effective. A voice and style are present.
3	The work is *somewhat creative*	The ideas/materials/methods used show signs of imagination and personal style.
2	The work is *not very creative*	The approach is trite and the ideas clichéd, leading to a flat and predictable performance.
1	The work is *uncreative*	The performance re-creates someone else's performance or relies exclusively on the models/algorithms/moves/recipes/templates/directions/materials provided.

(Source: https://grantwiggins.files.wordpress.com/2012/02/creative.pdf)

It's common for teachers to look for references in guiding standards documents for justification for teaching a theme or targeted body of knowledge or for pursuing specific student learning outcomes. It is no different with creativity. Because creativity is often associated with the arts and fun activities, seen by some as frivolous and not central to required, important learning, finding connections in standards documents is particularly reassuring for teachers who are determined make creativity an important part of what they pursue with their students. Those connections exist.

Creativity and Academic Standards

In her article titled "Six Ways the Common Core is Good for Students," published on the National Education Association website, author Cindy Long lists first that the "Common Core Puts Creativity Back in the Classroom." This amplifies an important reflection from a Massachusetts high school Math teacher, Peter Mili, who points out that a lot of teachers have fun, creative activities that they've fully developed and that are ready to go, but that they rarely find time to implement them because they are working in the era of standardized tests, the culture of accountability.

The Common Core promises to allow those activities to again see the light of day because, as Long notes, "the Common Core State Standards are just that—standards and not a prescribed curriculum. They may tell educators what students should be able to do by the end of a grade or course, but it's up to the educators to figure out how to deliver the instruction." And so, while specific instances in which the Common Core standards call for creativity by name are not in abundance, there is certainly opportunity within the standards for work that will tap and develop student creativity (Long, 2013).

Contrary to popular perception, the Common Core was designed to be less prescriptive than many states' previous standards. For example, the English language arts standards do not prescribe novel or nonfiction selections. Instead, they gradually push students to more deeply understand and reflect on what they read, using texts of the teacher's or district's choosing.

Likewise, Common Core mathematics standards are less concerned that students master a single prescribed approach to getting the right answer, and instead emphasize understanding why several ways to solve a problem correctly might work. Ideally, this gives students the ability to choose flexibly from different calculation and problem-solving strategies in the same way most of us do when we encounter math in real life.

While direct references to creativity in the Common Core standards may not be in abundance, there are some of broad importance. The English language arts anchor standards for college and career readiness for writing provide a good example of this.

> **English Language Arts Standards, College and Career Readiness Anchor Standards for Writing, 6 (CCSS.ELA-LITERACY.CCRA.W.6)**
>
> Use technology, including the Internet, to produce and publish writing and to interact and collaborate with others.

This anchor standard relates to a great many possible creativity-oriented literacy activities. In fact, the description could easily be applied to the practice of blogging.

An overall examination of the English Language Arts Common Core standards reveal a good number of standards that relate strongly to technology-supported activities to develop student creativity. Note that the verbs used to describe student activity in these may literally call for something other than creativity, but creativity can easily be inferred and understood as varieties of creative acts, for instance: "write, introduce, state, develop" and so on.

The Common Core Standards are readily available online at the Common Core State Standards Initiative website (corestandards.org). Table 8.3 offers a selection of the standards for English Language Arts (CCSS ELA) and mathematics (CCSS Mathematics).

Table 8.3: Common Core ELA and Mathematics Standards
with Suggested Activities to Foster Creativity

CCSS ELA Standards	SAMPLE ACTIVITIES AND APPROACHES TO PRODUCE WORK THAT ADDRESSES THE STANDARD.
CCSS.ELA-Literacy.W.5.1 **Write** opinion pieces on topics or texts, supporting a point of view with reasons and information.	Students select works of art from museum websites and write opinions about their meaning taking on the role of the artist to make the argument. They do web research to find supportive materials and background history on the artist and the work.
CCSS.ELA-Literacy.W.5.1.a **Introduce** a topic or text clearly, **state** an opinion, and **create** an organizational structure in which ideas are logically grouped to support the writer's purpose.	Use a variety of graphic organizers to visualize and brainstorm possible groupings of ideas. Conduct web research to locate similar pieces of writing on which to model a response and use a graphic organizer to plot and study their structure.
CCSS.ELA-Literacy.W.5.1.d **Provide** a concluding statement or section related to the opinion presented.	Conduct web research to locate similar pieces of writing on which to model a solution. Use a digital thesaurus to generate varieties of vocabulary on which to base a variety of concluding statements. Conduct an online survey to gather reactions to and interpretations of the opinion represented.
CCSS.ELA-Literacy.W.5.2 **Write** informative/explanatory texts to examine a topic and convey ideas and information clearly.	Use word processing functions to create a variety of versions of a text, using alternate vocabulary selections. Use an image search engine to locate images with which to illustrate the focus idea. Use flow chart resources to indicate the value, relationship, and flow of ideas.
CCSS.ELA-Literacy.W.5.2.a Introduce a topic clearly, **provide** a general observation and focus, and group related information logically; include formatting (e.g., headings), illustrations, and multimedia when useful to aiding comprehension.	Use word processing functions to visually differentiate and clarify the ideas expressed in text, and graphic organizer/flow chart functions to organize ideas and represent them in sequence and importance/value. Search for illustrations and media items. Use word processing functions to insert media items and browser/online content platforms (e.g., blogs) in which to embed multimedia items (e.g., MPG, MP3 files) and display them.
CCSS.ELA-Literacy.W.5.2.b **Develop** the topic with facts, definitions, concrete details, quotations, or other information and examples related to the topic.	Use search engines and online resources to locate relevant facts and quotes with which to enhance writing.

(table continued on next page)

CCSS ELA Standards	SAMPLE ACTIVITIES AND APPROACHES TO PRODUCE WORK THAT ADDRESSES THE STANDARD.
CCSS.ELA-Literacy.W.5.2.e **Provide** a concluding statement or section related to the information or explanation presented.	Students select cartoon panels from a library of comic strips selected and excerpted by teacher from published sources. They provide caption or dialog to end it, justifying their narration using available evidence in panel image or text
CCSS.ELA-Literacy.W.5.3 **Write** narratives to develop real or imagined experiences or events using effective technique, descriptive details, and clear event sequences.	Use timeline resources to depict events in sequence. Use word processing functions to write and place captions for images and bold text items placed on the timeline. Write and embed hyperlinks within the text captions and labels on the timeline, and/or transform locations on the timeline or graphics inserted to it as illustrations as links to informational websites.
CCSS.ELA-Literacy.W.5.3.a Orient the reader by establishing a situation and **introducing** a narrator and/or characters; organize an event sequence that unfolds naturally.	Use online animation, comic strip, or avatar resources to create and present a story. Use voice from text or digital audio recording resources to provide oral narration to tell a story or accompany images that tell a story.
CCSS.ELA-Literacy.W.5.3.b Use narrative techniques, such as dialogue, description, and pacing, to **develop** experiences and events or show the responses of characters to situations.	Use online comic strip resources to depict characters responding to situations, as well as their dialogue functions to indicate responses through text formatted and presented for that purpose.
CCSS.ELA-Literacy.W.5.3.e **Provide** a conclusion that follows from the narrated experiences or events.	Use search engines to research examples and commentary on similar experiences or text.
CCSS.ELA-Literacy.W.5.6 With some guidance and support from adults, use technology, including the Internet, to produce and publish writing as well as to interact and collaborate with others; demonstrate sufficient command of keyboarding skills to type a minimum of two pages in a single sitting.	Use blog resources, website resources, virtual publication resources, or media sharing sites to publish writing online and to distribute it to appropriate audiences.

CCSS ELA Standards	SAMPLE ACTIVITIES AND APPROACHES TO PRODUCE WORK THAT ADDRESSES THE STANDARD.
CCSS.ELA-Literacy.W.5.8 Recall relevant information from experiences or **gather** relevant information from print and digital sources; summarize or paraphrase information in notes and finished work, and provide a list of sources.	Use online collaboration resources (e.g., Google docs, web conferencing resources, online survey resources, etc.) to gather and generate informational material from a group of colleagues or targeted focus groups. Use search engines to locate sources of information. Use online bibliography resources to organize and format lists of resources.
CCSS Mathematics Standards	SAMPLE ACTIVITIES AND APPROACHES TO PRODUCE WORK THAT ADDRESSES THE STANDARD.
CCSS.Math. Content.5.MD.B.2 Make a line plot to display a data set of measurements in fractions of a unit (1/2, 1/4, 1/8). Use operations on fractions for this grade to solve problems involving information presented in line plots. *For example, given different measurements of liquid in identical beakers, find the amount of liquid each beaker would contain if the total amount in all the beakers were redistributed equally.*	Use the drawing functions of software and apps to create a line plot that is both expressive and communicates the mathematical idea of fractions in a linear fashion. Use digital drawing resources and/or use search engines to locate images with which to create illustrations of items that visually represent fractions.
CCSS.Math. Content.7.EE.B.4.a Solve word problems leading to equations of the form $px + q = r$ and $p(x + q) = r$, where p, q, and r are specific rational numbers. Solve equations of these forms fluently. Compare an algebraic solution to an arithmetic solution, identifying the sequence of the operations used in each approach. *For example, the perimeter of a rectangle is 54 cm. Its length is 6 cm. What is its width?*	Use image searches and digital drawing resources to locate and transform images to illustrate word problems so that other students will better understand them.

ISTE Standards

Another body of student learning standards that strongly relate to student creativity and its development are the ISTE Standards for Students. Again, as we consider the assessment and accountability issues around making the development of student creativity a significant part of the instructional program, we must look at student work and the application of creativity as students do things and produce things. Seen from that perspective, it is easy to see connections between such projects and all of the ISTE Standards for Students.

For instance, in response to the challenge that states, "Imagine and represent what a colony on a successful, functioning distant planet might be like," a group of students might conduct online research into an actual space colony project and/or Earth colonies from which they might extrapolate information and ideas for ones of the future. From the information they turn up they would have to parse good ideas from bad and work on problems that have not been solved as of yet. They might seek out input from experts by using appropriate "Ask an Expert" technologies, communicating effectively and in ways appropriate to the task while, in the process, keeping themselves safe and demonstrating good digital citizenship. They certainly might utilize a wide variety of digital resources. They might use the web to conduct research, use graphic organizers to consolidate and analyze the information they gather, contact others via email, use word processing–desktop publishing–slide presentation resources, as well as audio, video, and animation media to represent what they've learned and created. Finally, they might use online resources to publish their work as well as to distribute it to an audience and gather feedback from them.

In other words, in working through the processes and stages of their problems, students would likely touch or immerse themselves in things that relate to all of the ISTE standards.

Of the seven 2016 ISTE Standards for Students, several (2, 3, 4, 5, and 6) most clearly relate to student creativity, either in part or in whole. And it is easy to see how addressing the challenge just described would result in students addressing these standards strongly, both in the general sense, as communicated by the very names of these standards, and more specifically in terms of the various defining and clarifying descriptions of them.

2. DIGITAL CITIZEN

Students recognize the rights, responsibilities, and opportunities of living, learning, and working in an interconnected digital world, and they act and model in ways that are safe, legal, and ethical. Students:

b. engage in positive, safe, legal, and ethical behavior when using technology, including social interactions online or when using networked devices.

c. demonstrate an understanding of and respect for the rights and obligations of using and sharing intellectual property.

3. KNOWLEDGE CURATOR

Students critically curate a variety of resources using digital tools to construct knowledge, produce creative artifacts, and make meaningful learning experiences for themselves and others. Students:

a. plan and employ effective research strategies to locate information and other resources for their intellectual or creative pursuits.

b. curate information from digital resources using a variety of tools and methods to create collections of artifacts that demonstrate meaningful connections or conclusions.

4. INNOVATIVE DESIGNER

Student use a variety of processes within a design process to identify and solve problems by creating new, useful, or imaginative solutions. Students:

a. know and use use a deliberate design process for generating ideas, testing theories, creating innovative artifacts, or solving authentic problems.

b. select and use digital tools to plan and manage a design process that considers design constraints and calculated risks.

c. develop, test, and refine prototypes as part of a cyclical design process.

d. exhibit a tolerance for ambiguity, perseverance, and the capacity to work with open-ended problems.

5. COMPUTATIONAL THINKER

Students develop and employ strategies for understanding and solving problems in ways that leverage the power of technological methods to develop and test solutions. Students:

a. formulate problem definitions suited for technology-assisted methods such as data analysis, abstract models, and algorithmic thinking in exploring and finding solutions.

b. collect data or identify relevant data sets, use digital tools to analyze them, and represent data in various ways to facilitate problem-solving and decision-making.

c. break problems into component parts, extract key information, and develop descriptive models to understand complex systems or facilitate problem-solving.

    d. understand how automation works and use algorithmic thinking to develop a sequence of steps to create and test automated solutions.

6. CREATIVE COMMUNICATOR

Students communicate clearly and express themselves creatively for a variety of purposes using the platforms, tools, styles, formats, and digital media appropriate to their goals. Students:

    a. choose the appropriate platforms and tools for meeting the desired objectives of their creation or communication.

    b. create original works or responsibly repurpose or remix digital resources into new creations

    c. communicate complex ideas clearly and effectively by creating a variety of digital objects such as visualizations, models, or simulations.

    d. publish or present content that customizes the message and medium for their intended audiences.

National Core Arts Standards

While often associated with the arts, creativity is an area of learning and human capacity that is present in all areas of learning. It should be noted that standards in arts subjects clearly relate to creativity and it is useful to see how this is expressed in arts standards documents.

The National Core Arts Standards, a complex standards document, notes five arts areas: dance, media arts, music, theater, and visual arts. These standards are organized around the principle that student learning and performance are best viewed and understood through the lens of four principal standards: creating, performing/presenting/producing, responding, and connecting. While the first area is creating, in other words creativity itself, the other areas comprise the context in which creativity is possible, practical, and from which it derives meaning. Further, while these arts standards specifically reference five areas, it is easy to see student creative work done within the context of other subject areas as works of art, including those areas traditionally thought of as "academic" subjects, particularly if they are done, at least in part, as such.

National Core Arts Standards: Dance, Media Arts, Music, Theatre, and Visual Arts

ANCHOR STANDARD 1. Generate and conceptualize artistic ideas and work.

ANCHOR STANDARD 2. Organize and develop artistic ideas and work.

ANCHOR STANDARD 3. Refine and complete artistic work.

ANCHOR STANDARD 4. Analyze, interpret, and select artistic work for presentation.

ANCHOR STANDARD 5. Develop and refine artistic work for presentation.

ANCHOR STANDARD 6. Convey meaning through the presentation of artistic work.

ANCHOR STANDARD 7. Perceive and analyze artistic work.

ANCHOR STANDARD 8. Interpret intent and meaning in artistic work.

ANCHOR STANDARD 9. Apply criteria to evaluate artistic work.

ANCHOR STANDARD 10. Synthesize and relate knowledge and personal experiences to make art.

ANCHOR STANDARD 11. Relate artistic ideas and works with societal, cultural, and historical context to deepen understanding.

Source: www.nationalartsstandards.org/#sthash.edGWxkaD.dpuf

Partnership for 21st Century Learning Standards

While the Partnership for 21st Century Learning's document, the Framework for 21st Century Learning, isn't presented as a formal standards document, it does represent a strong statement about "student outcomes, the skills, knowledge, and expertise students should master to succeed in work and life in the 21st century."

An important section of framework titled "Learning and Innovation Skills" explains that "learning and innovation skills increasingly are being recognized as the skills that separate students who are prepared for increasingly complex life and work environments in the 21st century, and those who are not. A focus on creativity, critical thinking, communication and collaboration is essential to prepare students for the future."

Following are key elements from the Framework for 21st Century Learning. These may prove valuable in planning activities to develop and foster student creativity as well as in designing assessments to measure student achievement in this area.

CREATIVITY AND INNOVATION

Think Creatively

- Use a wide range of idea creation techniques (such as brainstorming)
- Create new and worthwhile ideas (both incremental and radical concepts)
- Elaborate, refine, analyze, and evaluate their own ideas in order to improve and maximize creative efforts

Work Creatively with Others

- Develop, implement, and communicate new ideas to others effectively
- Be open and responsive to new and diverse perspectives; incorporate group input and feedback into the work
- Demonstrate originality and inventiveness in work and understand the real world limits to adopting new ideas
- View failure as an opportunity to learn; understand that creativity and innovation is a long-term, cyclical process of small successes and frequent mistakes

Implement Innovations

- Act on creative ideas to make a tangible and useful contribution to the field in which the innovation will occur

CRITICAL THINKING AND PROBLEM SOLVING

Reason Effectively

- Use various types of reasoning (inductive, deductive, etc.) as appropriate to the situation

Use Systems Thinking

- Analyze how parts of a whole interact with each other to produce overall outcomes in complex systems

Make Judgments and Decisions

- Effectively analyze and evaluate evidence, arguments, claims and beliefs
- Analyze and evaluate major alternative points of view
- Synthesize and make connections between information and arguments

- Interpret information and draw conclusions based on the best analysis
- Reflect critically on learning experiences and processes

Solve Problems

- Solve different kinds of nonfamiliar problems in both conventional and innovative ways
- Identify and ask significant questions that clarify various points of view and lead to better solutions

Source: www.p21.org/about-us/p21-framework

INTERVIEW

Rose Reissman

Rose Reissman is a prominent literacy educator and author who lives and works in the New York City area. She has long worked in the area of student creativity, approaching it from the entry points of literacy instruction and project-based learning. She is founder of the Writing Institute program, which has been implemented in more than 130 schools.

MG: Why have you devoted so much of your long career to fostering student creativity?

RR: Because we are living in a 21st-century society, a period in which issues like global warming and pandemics come up frequently. And so, we had better educate creative citizens, people who can generate multiple responses to the issues of our day. In educating creative citizens educators should be implementing the things that Howard Gardner wrote about, activities and projects that engage students from his multiple intelligences perspective for instance, as well as the things understood from the perspective of social and emotional learning.

MG: Where do you recommend teachers begin in strategizing to make student creativity an important part of what they offer in their classrooms?

RR: Importantly, there are elements of the typical instructional program in the average school that can be used to nurture creativity. For instance, there are: student robotics, school newspapers, student-produced news shows done over the school PA system or online, the school choir, museum in a school projects, plays and performances.

Ensuring that such activities foster creativity, though, requires that the teacher model the creative act for students. Modeling is an essential approach. Also, a discovery oriented, "walk about" approach to guiding students to and through creative projects is effective. I like to take kids outside the school building and have them identify stories, reconsider discarded objects, sketch, eavesdrop, do a sound collage with an audio recorder or use a mobile phone to take videos, that sort of thing. There needs to be an anticipated product that the students will create, as well. Importantly, what most teachers are looking for from their students—a single, correct answer to a simple, finite question—is counterproductive. And so, a shift to open-ended solutions and responses from students, at least for some of the work they do in a classroom, is necessary. Also, there's a relationship between differentiation in instruction and creativity, as students may be called on to provide alternate varieties of responses when working in the context of differentiated instruction. Further, creativity can only be nurtured in a positive, warm, receptive, exciting learning environment.

MG: What about creative writing? Do schools foster creativity through teaching students to write? And what about the Common Core?

RR: Creative writing used to be considered a key part of teaching writing and today some may think creative writing died a sad death. However, under the Common Core, which is very much in place and alive, we're supposed to teach argument, we're supposed to teach persuasive writing, we're supposed to teach 21st Century critical thinking, and anybody who does that really has to teach creative writing, although currently it may often not be labeled with that name. Although the Common Core ELA standards involve a shift away from fiction to informational, nonfiction tests, as any lawyer or journalist would tell you, the act of generating effective arguments and of persuading people through language is a creative art. It's about generating original, unanticipated and perhaps, surprising connections between ideas and things. On the other side of this discussion, while we still want students to read fiction, we also want them to see and understand how writing novels involves the author both mining his own life and experience and doing research for material on which to base his works of fiction. If you think deeply about this you'll realize that all fiction is based on life. The more information that you put into a work of fiction the more real it is. If a novel were to be disconnected from reality it would be awful.

MG: And what about essay writing and nurturing student voice?

RR: Some folks wonder about whether or not teaching functional writing, the templated five-paragraph essay, for instance, will stifle creativity. Creativity is putting

your own take or twist on a particular formula. Creativity, particularly in writing, is not necessarily creating things that have never been approached by others previously, it is putting one's own bent on a format that may be well known by virtue of others having created wonderfully within it. The wonderful thing about the essay is that it is a format that one can make one's own, a format that if seen correctly supports one in making it his own. Make it your own by using a phrase or a sound that is your own style and that gives us, the readers, some unique information about who you are, but that still conforms to the accepted understanding of the format. Teachers really must provide students an opportunity to develop and exercise their authentic voice; that's an important part of fostering creativity, to express yourself and do it through your authentic voice.

MG: Can we nurture student creativity and still comply with the demands of assessment and accountability?

RR: Presentation of knowledge is an opportunity for creativity within the context of regular subject-based instruction. Required grade level and high school exit exams ask students to explain science and math concepts, and within that framework, students can add their own personality as they creatively display and present, knowledge.

Student publishing is a wonderful dimension of teaching and learning and by assigning students to produce something that will be published, teachers are sparking their creativity. The dynamic of presenting a student learning product brings out the creative in students. To that end, I not only engage students in producing products, like author fan websites, but I also create opportunities for students get themselves and their work before real audiences. Yes, I have students present to peers in school, but I also arrange for my students to go out into the community—to Senior Centers and even to graduate school teaching classes—places where the authenticity and the gravitas of the audience communicates to the students the importance of what they are doing.

MG: How about recommending some resources, digital or other, that you use to support the kind of student creativity focused approaches and activities you like to do with students and their teachers.

RR: I find all the following to be very useful: digital cameras, the Polaroid Snap Instant Digital Camera, digital audio recorders, traditional art supplies, over-sized/poster-sized printers and glossy, art-quality paper, Adobe InDesign desktop publishing software, Claymation software, and trifold poster boards.

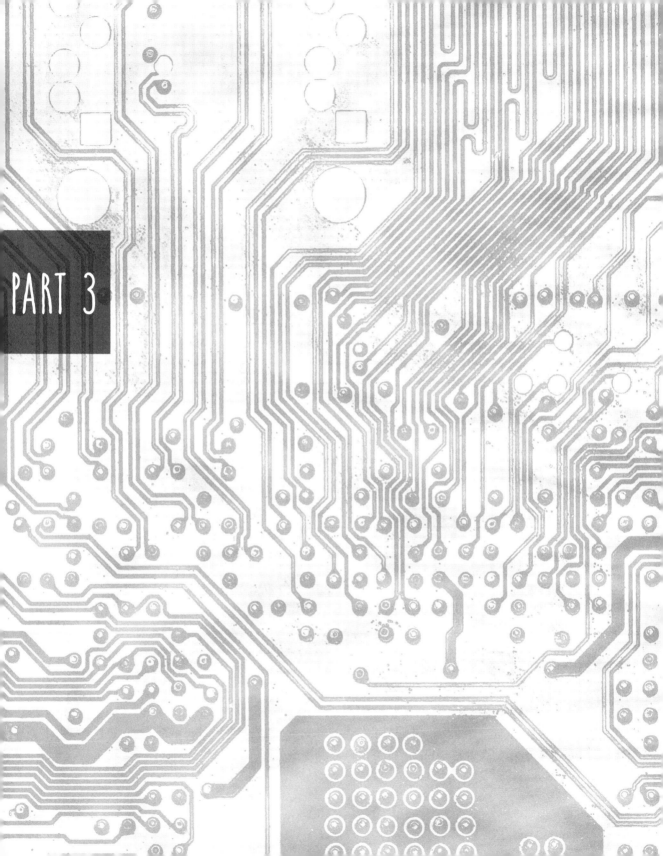

PART 3

Teaching
CREATIVITY

Inspiration is for amateurs. The rest of us just get to work.

—Chuck Close, Artist

C an creativity be learned? Can it be taught? Better yet, can we encourage and support students in developing it? Over the years a great deal has been written about teaching and learning creativity. Suffice it to say that a very long-term stream of opinion, much of it informed by focused direct experience or research, indicates that creativity can be taught, or at the very least, nurtured, encouraged, and expanded through focused efforts. In this section, approaches and lesson ideas are shared to give you a sample of these efforts. Chapter 9 shares some background and pedagogy for teaching creativity. Chapter 10 shares instructional approaches for teaching creativity. Chapter 11 offers lesson ideas and examples of activities to encourage creativity. Chapter 12 addresses teaching creativity across the curriculum and shares suggestions for teaching creativity within specific subject matter areas.

Chapter 9

Background and Pedagogy

Research reports, and articles explaining them, emerge with some degree of regularity indicating that yes, creativity can be learned. In the article "Who Says Creativity Can't Be Learned?" Tina Seelig, the executive director of the Stanford Technology Ventures Program (the entrepreneurship center at Stanford University School of Engineering), states:

> We are all naturally creative and, like every other skill, some people have more natural talent than others. However, everyone can increase his or her creativity, just as everyone can increase his or her musical or athletic ability, with appropriate training and focused practice. We can all learn tools and techniques that enhance creativity, and build environments that foster innovation. (Seelig, 2012)

In his BBC article "Can You Learn to Be Creative?" science writer, Colin Barras, discusses teaching creativity with Gerard Puccio, chair of the International Center for Studies in Creativity at Buffalo State in New York, concluding that "...creativity techniques are not going to turn an average kid into a young Einstein or Picasso—everyone accepts that you can't teach genius. It's more about encouraging the day-to-day creative thinking that can make students and an adult workforce more productive." Puccio calls it creativity with a little "c" and he's convinced it's a talent we all possess, saying, "You're human and you have an imagination. You are wired to be creative." (Barras, 2014)

Puccio holds that creativity follows prescribed phases or steps. They are: clarifying (defining the challenge or problem accurately and precisely), ideating (brain storming and conceiving as many possible responses or solutions to the problem as possible), developing (fleshing out likely solutions with details as well as tweaking and redirecting as the solution's evolving form suggests), and implementing (applying the developed solution in a real-world context to test and evaluate its adequacy and quality at completion). Examples of how these phases align with instructional activities are provided in the aforementioned BBC article. Toward the end of the article, Barras presents an essential understanding about teaching creativity relayed to him by Puccio, one that all teachers should grapple with as they integrate the development of creativity into the other areas of instruction they provide their students:

> No one in creativity research argues that children should give free rein to their imagination at the cost of understanding a subject. After all, you can't think outside the box until you fully understand what's inside the box. But with 21st century firms emphasizing the value of creativity in their employees, it's important that teachers are allowed to value the trait in their students too—which is something that today's curriculums often discourage," says Puccio. (Barras 2014)

Moving forward from the position that creativity can be learned, educators will logically wrestle with the question of whether or not it can be taught. "Taught" connotes a very active role from the teacher, and surely this is part of the picture,

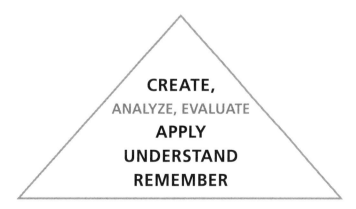

Figure 9.1: A representation of Bloom's New Taxonomy of the Cognitive Domain (by the author) places creativity at the top of a pyramid of cognitive learning behaviors.

although the things that teachers may do to foster student creativity may include many types of support, nourishment, and instruction that are more subtle and passive in character than the classic image of hands-on, active teaching. Among other things this may include:

- establishing a physical and virtual environment that provides space to display creative projects to the class community, as well as a variety of resources and tools with which to create them

- providing personalized feedback for work in progress, particularly reactions, reflections, and suggestions that are non-judgmental and collaborative; and

- modeling creative behaviors and attitudes in one's own work and approach to solving problems.

Approaches to Teaching Creativity

One approach and distinction worth understanding is that of teaching creativity versus teaching about creativity. The former ultimately will require, at least in part, direct hands-on/minds-on creative work and experiences. Still, reflecting on what the creative process is, both before, during, and after personal experience in a creative effort or project, will add to the development of creativity. Having students learn about the creative process through studying the lives and works of individuals whose accomplishments are strongly associated with their creativity will make for a richer and more worthwhile learning experience. A wealth of books, articles, and videos can serve for this purpose. YouTube offers many interviews of creative individuals who speak about their creativity. Here are some examples worth looking at to get the idea.

Interview with Japanese Artist Hiroaki Kano at Art Stage Singapore 2014 (youtube. com/watch?v=Zj6R6QpW-BI)

Interview with songwriter Adele, Live from the Artists Den (February 25, 2011) (youtube.com/watch?v=XE0_xCcfbxM)

Interview with the author Judy Blume (youtube.com/watch?v=91eJiPqVOAM)

Bringing out Creativity in a Standards-Based Environment

The SmartBrief cover summary of Nicholas Provenzano's Edutopia blog article titled "Creativity in the Classroom" announces that this high school English teacher believes that "it's still possible to integrate creativity into classroom lessons while also preparing students for standardized tests." In his article, he advises: "Standardized tests are a reality where I teach, but I still find creativity time for my students."

He shares his three favorite strategies for doing this: open-ended projects, genius hour/20% time, and creative team building. (Provenzano, 2015)

OPEN-ENDED PROJECTS

Provenzano provides some basic guidelines for students to follow. He provides a topic, and then asks them to create a presentation based on it. He develops a rubric with them, as well. He insists that for each successive project of this type that they do for his class, they employ a different medium and format. According to Provenzano, "With an open-ended project, the students get to choose the type of project they want to create and the rubric by which they'll be graded. Students are excited to explore different passions and present their discoveries in ways that are comfortable to them." (Provenzano, 2015)

GENIUS HOUR OR 20% TIME

"Depending on what level you teach, you can devote one hour a day or one day a week over a set time period for letting students explore something they're passionate about. This allows them to attempt things they might not try outside of school because of time constraints. By encouraging students to work on something they care about in school, they begin making connections between their passions and their learning." (Provenzano, 2015)

Provenzano explained that one of his students built a boat with his grandfather during the school year. The student spent his class time researching the different aspects of boat building and blogging his reflections on the entire process. This resulted in him greatly improving his writing and key research skills by working on something creative that mattered to him.

CREATIVE TEAM BUILDING

According to Provenzano, "a classroom should be a collaborative environment where students work together to support everyone's learning. A great way to set the tone is by starting the year with some fun team-building exercises."

He explains that his favorite team task is a simple one taking a class period. He assigns students to build the tallest freestanding tower they can using small marshmallows and raw pasta that he provides. He explains: "Once the students have the supplies and an understanding of what you expect, sit back and watch the creativity explode. Solid communication skills and planning are needed to be successful. In fact, all of the skills that students have picked up in the classroom can be seen when you give them a problem and time to solve it" (Provenzano, 2015).

Divergent Thinking

In his Edutopia post, "Fuel Creativity in the Classroom With Divergent Thinking," art teacher Stacey Goodman focuses on the phenomenon of divergent thinking to make creativity an important outcome of his classroom. Mr. Goodman says that:

> Divergent thinking refers to the way the mind generates ideas beyond proscribed expectations and rote thinking—what is usually referred to "thinking outside the box," and is often associated with creativity. Convergent thinking, on the other hand, requires one to restrict ideas to those that might be correct or the best solution to a problem …. Studies suggest that, as children, our divergence capability operate at a genius level, but that our ability to think divergently decreases dramatically as we become adults. (Goodman, 2015)

Goodman shares a wide variety of instructional strategies, many of which promise to work in teaching creativity in the context of art class and across the curriculum, as well. The following are among his strategies.

REVERSING THE QUESTION/ANSWER PARADIGM

The premise of this strategy is simple: Instead of asking questions to which there is a correct answer, ask students to create the problem. Students pose their problem by first tapping into their own wishes and goals that might have real-life results or be largely theoretical. Questions that encourage students to think divergently might be: "How can we grow vegetables without using pesticides?" And, "How can we feed the world's population in a sustainable way?"

INQUIRY-BASED FEEDBACK

Instead of value-based feedback, inquiry coupled by deep observation encourages a more open-ended and in-depth approach for evaluating students' work. Students are encouraged to minimize expressing their likes and dislikes, but to first spend at least two minutes silently observing, and then asking questions prefixed by phrases such as, "I noticed that …" "why …," and "how …."

ENCOURAGE PLAY AND MANAGE FAILURE

When failure is framed by reflection and iteration and less by penalty and closure, we are more likely to loosen up in our efforts and be less afraid to make mistakes. Once we are less afraid to make mistakes, we open up the environment for play and experimentation. In my community art class, I prepare my students to take risks in their own projects by creating one-day exercises in which they engage with the public in a safe but unpredictable way.

ART STRATEGIES

I use a few art strategies such as collage, readymade, and pareidolia to open up the divergent thinking part of the students' brains. This allows students to become less concerned by exact interpretation and become more open to poetry, metaphor, and dream imagery in general. (Goodman, 2015)

Fostering Creativity through Personal Channels

One important approach to cultivating creativity is to help individual students find an area of creativity to which they relate in particular, one that seems to be a natural fit. A person may find it easy to be creative as a writer, but not as a musician; or as a visual artist, but not as a dancer ... choosing a supportive vehicle for creativity that seems a natural and effective fit can help a great deal.

For nearly a decade I held the position of visual arts teacher at the East Harlem Performing Arts School. This was a school for students who had an interest or affinity for learning through the arts. In addition to visual art, every student was scheduled to take a music, a dance, and a drama class. Even though it wasn't specifically designed for them, inevitably some highly talented and accomplished students who had an eye on the performing arts as a profession enrolled in the school. Several of them actually went on to become internationally famous stars appearing on the stage or in major films. Interestingly, while these students were rarely a problem, they tended to hang back and participate only marginally in the arts classes that didn't teach an art type to which they didn't have a particular affinity, although they may have been masterful at the ones they did relate to.

Creativity should not be considered something that belongs exclusively in the art or music room or perhaps, in classes where creative writing is taught. All teachers can find places and opportunities where creativity can be made part of what's taught. If we fail to make this happen, students will likely infer from their school experience that creativity is not part of the mainstream of human intellectual efforts, that it is a phenomenon exclusively associated with tangential areas, like the arts. The disciplines that we teach, and about which we communicate to students a strong sense of importance—math, science, social studies, and the like—all were developed through acts of creativity. Creativity should be included and celebrated in these subject areas and not marginalized as something separate from the so-called "academic" areas of learning and which should be engaged in only occasionally for special reasons.

Developing student creativity in the classroom (and beyond) requires teachers to address the following areas:

ENVIRONMENT

This involves both the physical environment and the culture and atmosphere in which students work and grow as individuals. Not only do students need the proverbial "clean, well-lighted place," one that will support their needs to concentrate and to collaborate, to tinker and work and experiment, but a space that provides for storage of their projects and the resources with which they create them and areas to present and exhibit them. The atmosphere should be a supportive one. One that emphasizes process over product as its core value. One that allows for and honors mistakes and false starts. One that elicits many ideas. One that celebrates creative work and encourages more of it on an ongoing basis.

ACTIVITIES

Creativity is not likely to be taught as a separate, discreet subject. The common organizational structure of schools is such that, if this were to be the approach taken, a creativity class would be offered as a minor, as an extra class, or strictly as an afterschool activity. The great value to be had, both in the level of creativity learning achieved and in reaping the benefits of creative work's impact on the whole of the educational experience, is from integrating creativity-oriented work into the various content subject area classes and across the curriculum. Consequently, student creativity is accomplished through work on projects and activities, and in understanding and moving away from the traditional reading, lecture, whole group discussion, and quiz format of instruction.

RESOURCES

Students need access to the materials and resources required to produce creative products and performances. These might include things to support activity in writing, making visual art, music, theater, science and engineering experiments, electronics and robotics, video and audio production. Failure to provide students with needed resources or providing resources to accommodate just one or a few areas would be to skew their learning and understanding significantly. Fortunately, today's world of digital resources has evolved so that students who have access to connected computing devices (e.g., desktops, laptops, tablets, smartphones, and so on) are able to acquire the resources they need to create. As well, they can find the "how to" tutorial information they need to effectively use them.

A few resources of particular interest for getting a snapshot overview of ideas, opportunities, resources, and practices to develop student creativity include the following:

Remake Learning (remakelearning.org)

PBS: How to Be Creative | Off Book (video) (tinyurl.com/z8lhd8e)

PBS:Creativity in Science (text lesson plan): (tinyurl.com/z8lhd8e)

Denver Art Museum Creativity Resource for Teachers: (tinyurl.com/jxltac8)

LEARN NC: Fostering creativity and innovation in the science classroom: (learnnc. org/lp/pages/7028)

Student Creativity: Zaiya's Whitehouse Film Festival Submission: (youtube.com/watch?v=Clug7DAUeG4)

Chapter 10

Instructional Approaches to Teaching Creativity

This chapter explores a body of important approaches to teaching and learning that can be instrumental in fostering and developing student creativity.

Project-Based Learning and Creativity

Project-based learning (PBL) is one of the clearest and most effective approaches by which student creativity, innovation, and related skills can be developed. There's a natural connection, although for a PBL project to produce such outcomes it will have to be planned with this result in mind.

The connections between PBL and the desired learning outcome of increased creativity understandings and skills can be strong. The design of most PBL projects not only calls for students to create a product and/or performance as an integral part of the learning experience, but for the targeted learning to be focused and generated by their creations, the products and performances that result from their efforts and that demonstrate their learning.

In short, in a typical PBL-based unit, the teacher sets a learning challenge for a class, one that provides a theme and sets parameters for how students are to investigate it. The teacher also establishes how and what students may create in response to the challenge and to demonstrate what they've learned. Many areas of required curriculum can be addressed through student exploration of such themes, using the PBL approach as a method for learning them.

The core of the learning experience involves students creating either a product (e.g., an illustrated book, a museum-style exhibition, a video or podcast) or a performance (e.g., a skit or play, the performance of a song, or a dramatic oral presentation to an audience). In order to create their product or performance, students must first narrow the teacher-provided theme down to a specific subject that embraces their own particular interests, and then they must learn about it as a way to inform the product or performance they will create based on it. Learning may involve library or web-based research, independent information gathering, interviewing or oral history discovery, and reflection on the theme-based items they've discovered. Students work on their creation until the criteria for learning and for products and performances (provided at the outset of the project) have been met or exceeded. Finally, students present it to an audience, which may be their peer classmates, the general population of the school, or even beyond that to parents and interested members of a larger community. It should be noted that in a variety of ways—in doing research, in preparing their products, in sharing them with their audience, and in gathering audience feedback to better understand their project learning experience and to target for next step learning experiences—technology is a facilitator. Indeed, without technology such projects would be difficult, if not impossible, to do practically or to the level of richness now common in PBL experiences.

Further, the PBL project process and its elements are clearly aligned with the numerous writing, design/engineering, innovation, and creativity processes described elsewhere in this book.

Essential PBL Project Design Elements

On its website (bie.org), the Buck Institute for Education provides its Essential Project Design Elements Checklist. This tool supports teachers in designing projects. Adhering to it assures teachers that their projects are grounded in and provide for a sufficient level of learning types best handled by PBL. The criteria included are:

- key knowledge, understanding, and success skills
- challenging problem or question
- sustained inquiry
- authenticity

- student voice & choice

- reflection

- critique & revision

- public product

A good number of these (public product, student voice & choice, and critique & revisions, for instance) clearly and strongly relate to developing student creativity. While other frameworks given in this book are expressed in stages or phases, the value giving characteristics of activities and the creativity-based learning they precipitate listed by the Buck Institute are much the same.

This understanding of a sequence of learning project stages is clearly illustrated, for instance, in the chapter titled "The Nine Steps of Project-Based Learning" of the book *Teachers as Classroom Coaches* (ASCD, 2006). This chapter provides the following list of steps or phases of a PBL learning experience.

1. The teacher-coach **sets the stage for students with real-life samples** of the projects they will be doing.

2. Students **take on the role of project designers**, possibly establishing a forum for display or competition.

3. Students **discuss and accumulate the background information** needed for their designs.

4. The teacher-coach and students **negotiate the criteria for evaluating the projects**.

5. Students **accumulate the materials** necessary for the project.

6. Students **create their projects**.

7. Students **prepare to present their projects**.

8. Students **present their projects**.

9. Students **reflect on the process and evaluate the projects** based on the criteria established in Step 4.

(Stix & Hrbek, 2006)

In comparing the two frameworks just described, one that lists design elements of learning projects and one that lists project steps, we can see that they both communicate essentially the same thing. For instance, in project Step 2 ("Students take on the role of project designers") relates directly to the design element "student voice

114

& choice" on the Essential Project Design Elements Checklist. Further, project Step 8 ("Students present their projects") can be seen as another way of saying "public product." And project Step 9 ("Students reflect on the process and evaluate the projects") is much the same thing as "critique & revision."

One of the great opportunities for teachers when addressing an area of required material is that they can teach that unit by having students explore and discover that area through guided and supported—but independent—research, investigation, and reflection. The focus here is to help students create an original product that communicates and demonstrates what they've learned, that demonstrates their original reflections and "aha" moments, and draws (possibly) feedback from others that, in turn, fuels further reflection and understanding.

Importantly, technology is essential to practical, successful PBL implementation. Common projects done currently, as well as the resources students commonly use to create them, are all closely associated with technology use. A few examples include book trailers, which are a popular alternative to the classic textbook report done using digital video and uploaded to media sharing sites like YouTube; student original comic strips, which are done with online comic strip resources; and student-created math video games that are made using a free online game creation resource like Gamestar Mechanic (gamestarmechanic.com).

Robotics and Creativity

In the 2015 article "Preparing Students for the Robotic Revolution" (OEB News Portal) Charles Fadel, founder of the Center for Curriculum Redesign and a visiting practitioner at Harvard's Graduate School of Education, states: "The only way for humans to succeed in the race against the machine is to "upskill'—and that means focusing on creativity."

He goes on to say: "While robots may be capable of incremental creativity, they cannot think outside the box …. Incremental creativity is just improving on something, but radical creativity is thinking something up." (Fadel, 2015)

According to the article, Fadel believes that truly original thinking is robot-proof. Thus robotics-based learning becomes doubly valuable for today's students. Not only does this learning develop their creativity directly, as they are challenged to conceive and develop robots as solutions to needs and problems, but it prepares them for a future in which robots may extend our creative abilities by their handling some creative chores for us as part of our creative process.

Instead of having students memorize facts like state capitals, something that is easily searchable online, students should focus on learning how to learn. Schools should teach students how to take facts, skills, and concepts and apply them to real-world problems.

Student robotics addresses that understanding of education effectively, providing an approach to instruction that satisfies those difficult-to-implement goals with a body of ready-to-go practice.

Observing students who have been set free to explore the possibilities of a robotics kit is to watch them become intrigued with and inspired by the materials and the possibilities they represent. Students experiment, draw conclusions, and generally inform and educate themselves and one another (yes, robotics makes a valuable social learning platform) about how they work and what they can do.

Figure 10.1 A team of students presenting at a robotics competition

There are many varieties of classroom-practical robotics materials currently on the market for prices that schools find affordable. Some are already complete robots that students program and then operate. Others come in kits from which students put the robots together. Others allow students to come up with original robot concepts and designs, construct them from parts provided by the kits, and then program and run them. Students can watch how their ideas come to life by way of their robot's real-world performance. The likely contender for the most favored kits by students and schools so far is the Lego student robotics family of products. (See the book *Getting Started with Lego Robotics*, published by ISTE, which supports students in participating in and acquiring this full complement of robotics skills and learning.)

In essence, such kits put students in the creative mindset occupied by today's engineers and technology entrepreneurs by supporting them with materials that allow them to actually build the things they imagine. These products support students in discovering what's possible and why via the unique marriage of concept, mechanics, digital electronics, and software that are provided through robots. The kits are practical, too, in that the materials and robots in various stages of completion are durable, storable, and reusable for school group after school group, and for robot project after robot project.

Student-created robots aren't solely about imagining real-world machines with which to address real-world needs and problems. There is an expressive side to them, too. For instance, the Hummingbird Robotics Kit from BirdBrain Technologies offers students the guidance and resources necessary in order to create robots designed as art works, creations that can be seen as being expressive, kinetic sculptures.

On a similar note, in the Classroom Robotics blog (classroomrobotics.blogspot.com) I included a passage about a robot-based, informative, museum-style exhibit on the ecology of sea turtles that was presented at the 2014 ISTE Conference by students from a school in Cancun, Mexico. In the display, hand-drawn student artwork was skillfully paired with Lego robotics-built machines that moved throughout the exhibit simulating the movements and travels of sea turtles. Thus, for the technology savvy students who put this exhibit together, and who added a little personal creativity to extend the manufacturer-provided capabilities, these robotics materials allowed them to create in ways that reflected what they admire in the real world. A trip to a theme park or interactive museum will turn up many instructive, illustrative uses of robotics, and young people today are anxious to try their hand at such things (Gura, 2014).

Another variety of robot/creativity connection is the Art Bot. Those who have investigated student robotics will recognize that this is a well-established type of robot for students to create. Students address the challenge, "How can I design and build a robot that will draw?" and then come up with their best solution.

Part of such an activity would logically include a demonstration of the Art Bot in action. Thus in this variety of activity the design of the robot is simply one dimension of the challenge. The other half, and perhaps the richer one, is realized in the next phase of the project: programming the robot to actually draw a design imagined by the robot's creator as it moves about on a table top and brings a marker or crayon in contact with a paper. This activity involves a number of levels of understanding, a wide variety of robotics skills, and importantly, a good deal of imagination and problem solving.

An online search will turn up a good number of videos of robots constructed by students as Art Bots, as well as the kind and level of performance they are capable of. A couple of worthwhile examples:

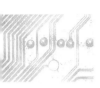

Art Bot–Student Innovation from Robo Station (youtube.com/watch?v=Ks6A_SxEbQw)

Arduino Draw Bot Creation (youtube.com/watch?v=0qnOl9tUZ1g)

Lego NXT Drawing Robot (youtube.com/watch?v=dl8CIaQidF0)

Lego Mindstorms NXT Writing Robot (youtube.com/watch?v=DFOvXlj-t3k)

Importantly, the meaningful learning in such projects does not end simply with creating the robot. By having it perform, and documenting that performance, students can be guided to ponder some important philosophical questions, such as: Can a robot be an artist? Is robot art really art? What's the difference? Of course, students can be asked these questions without actually building a robot. However, the level of commitment to answering such questions and the authority with which they answer them cannot be achieved any other way.

Yet another creative dimension to student robotics can be seen in the Lego Education WeDo kits. These kits are designed primarily for elementary aged students. Storytelling is one of the prime anticipated applications of robots created with these kits as students imagine, design, construct, program, and operate robots for this purpose. We might see this as programmed, automated puppets, things that bridge the realms of language, storytelling, imagination, and technology somewhat seamlessly to produce rich learning environments and activities for young students.

Such projects offer us an opportunity to move from an approach to instructional organization in our schools that conceives of instruction as being offered in *either* STEM subjects *or* humanities-oriented subjects to one defined as STEAM, the "A" in STEAM standing for arts, which are fully integrated with the STEM subjects. As a result, the place of robotics as support for student-creative efforts in the context of humanities will further establish itself.

Creative Activities Students Engage in with Robotics

- Students explore robotics materials themselves, making discoveries about how robots work and making important connections between components, components in groupings working together, and the possibilities for applying components.

- Students conceive of robots to perform tasks based on real-world needs and applications.

- Students conceive of robots as fanciful expressions and ideas beyond robots' functions as real-world solutions to needs and problems.

- Students design robots in order to realize their robot conceptions and engage in creative problem solving to make them work.

- Students document and present their robot creations in competitions, demonstrations, and a variety of media products.

In the article "Robots Rule as Competition Season Heats Up," Chris Bradshaw, chief marketing officer and senior vice president for reputation, consumer, and education for the software company Autodesk states:

> One of the biggest complaints we get from our professional customers is that when they go to hire, the kids coming out of college have degrees, they're smart, but they don't have a lot of creativity …. We're training kids from five or six years old to believe that every answer is either A, B, C, or D—one of the circles. [During] most all of K–12 and college, you're filling in dots that say, "There is one right answer to this question." When you go to these robotic competitions and you see every team with the same kit and same instructions and competing with the same rulebook, there will not be even two robots that look even remotely alike. This notion of A, B, C, or D evaporates in this environment. You get kids learning that many solutions are possible. Many solutions work. (Schaffhauser, 2012)

In essence, he is stating that robotics is inherently a creative area of human work and learning.

Play, Curiosity, Wonder, Imagination, Personal Expression, and Creativity

Many have observed that our schools have become business-like environments in which young students are expected to work tirelessly, remaining "on task" as they go about the serious business of acquiring important skills and bodies of knowledge in preparation for higher education and the world of work and careers beyond school. Apart from issues of child well-being associated with holding youngsters accountable for continued and productive engagement in serious, measurable learning, there is the alternate concern about the type of learning that often is the predominant or exclusive variety pursued in such environments. Much has been written about the value and need for play, curiosity, wonder, imagination, personal expression, and creativity as part of child development (and by extension, the development of adolescents and young adults, as well).

In her 2015 Edutopia blog post titled "Curiosity: The Force Within a Hungry Mind," Marilyn Price-Mitchell, PhD, a developmental psychologist, explains that: "Psychologists view curiosity as a life force, vital to happiness, intellectual growth, and well being …. The greatest advantage of curiosity lies in its power to motivate learning in areas of life and work that are meaningful to the learner. It points students toward the knowledge, skills, relationships, and experiences that they need to live full and productive lives." Among the list of 10 Ways to Stimulate a Student's Curiosity that she provides is "Encourage students to tinker. Tinkering might be constructive play with feelings, concepts, ideas, and materials. How can students create a new widget, essay, blog article, poem, science experiment, service, or product from their explorations? Tinkering with materials, thoughts, and emotions stimulates curiosity and leads to innovative outcomes." (Price-Mitchell, 2015)

Student robotics is a classroom-proven, practical way to establish a learning environment that supports opportunities for high quality student tinkering. It is a variety of tinkering, as well, that is connected to more formal areas of learning. Robotics, however, is only one of many approaches that can be used to support student tinkering as a stimulus to creativity. These include programming online avatar resources like Voki and writing programs for robots with object-based languages like the Lego NXT and WeDo. Even straightforward curiosity-centric activities like creating photo collages in word processing programs—a process that involves inserting photos, sizing them, experimenting with their placement and relationship to the whole—can stimulate creativity.

In a related Edutopia post titled "Embracing Student Creativity with a Wonder Shelf", former high school math teacher Refranz Davis describes how over a period of years she developed a classroom resource that she sees as addressing her students important needs: "It was important for me to create a learning space that welcomed on-demand wonder and exploration …. With a few containers, manipulatives, and supplies, along with some technology, I created a space that my students would go on to name 'the wonder shelves'." (Davis, 2014)

Whatever format wonder shelves take, however, their equivalents uniquely adhere to the flavor and culture of a specific classroom; the point is that providing a "space" and resources for this purpose, to provide the opportunity for students to be curious, to wonder, to tinker and try things, to relate them to specific formal learning or to explore independent of it, is a dimension of learning not well served by schools currently. But they do represent an important need, one that will pay big dividends for students today and society in the future.

Wonderopolis

One resource of particular note that addresses the need for students to indulge their capacity for wonder and to reflect on it, and to make it the focus of ongoing learning efforts, is the online learning website Wonderopolis (wonderopolis.org). The About page announces "Wonder is for everyone. It can happen anywhere and at anytime. Connecting the learning we do in our schools, our homes, and our communities, Wonderopolis walks the line between formal and informal education. Each day, we pose an intriguing question and explore it in a variety of ways. Our approach both informs and encourages new questions, sparking new paths of wonder and discovery in family and classroom settings."

FIGURE 10.2 Interactive questions are one feature of the Wonderopolis website.

In essence, Wonderopolis is a socially networked online resource in which community members post things they wonder about, get answers to their wonder-based questions from experts and other community members, learn from the questions of peers and others, and take advantage of a body of supports and resources to further their wondering and learning from it. Wonderopolis is extremely user friendly and free. It is the sort of resource from which creativity-minded teachers can find support for their students or confidently have them reap benefits on their own.

Entrepreneurship and Creativity

One context in which student creativity may be developed that is particularly aligned with the ways that individuals are creative in the world of work and careers is entrepreneurship. Just as business people must create their own business models by picking and choosing from established practices in addition to creating original approaches (something that relates to the mashup—the freshly created, unique collection and arrangement of existing or established elements), student entrepreneurship involves making similar efforts.

In the article "Creating the Entrepreneurial Mindset in 21st Century Schools," Dr. Yong Zhao poses the question that while we admire, envy, and celebrate entrepreneurs like Henry Ford, Thomas Edison, Steve Jobs, Richard Branson, and Mark Zuckerberg, our society produces very few of them. He states, "Why, you may ask, is the 'entrepreneurial mindset' missing in our society in general and among our youth in particular? That our schools don't teach entrepreneurship seems to be a logical answer." (Zhao, 2014)

In probing for insights into this question and imagining possible solutions, Dr. Zhao states further,

> Entrepreneurship is fundamentally about the desire to solve problems creatively. The foundation of entrepreneurship—creativity, curiosity, imagination, risk-taking, and collaboration—is just like the ideas of engineering .... To cultivate the entrepreneurial mindset cannot be achieved by simply adding another course to teach entrepreneurship to the existing paradigm. We now need a new education paradigm—entrepreneur-oriented education, instead of the employee-oriented education. (Zhao, 2014)

It follows, then, that by teaching creativity as part and parcel of entrepreneurship we can develop in students the understandings and skills that will be authentic to real-world needs, preparing students well to succeed in it. And we will be able to provide activities and experiences directed at developing creativity that will fit and function well within the context of practical learning.

Virtual Enterprises

The virtual enterprise approach to immersing students in a creativity-oriented business experience offers ideas for activities and contexts in which students will tap their creativity to participate in entrepreneurship. The website of the New York City Department of Education advises that:

> The Virtual Enterprise involves students in every aspect of a business, including human resources, accounting, product development, production, distribution, marketing and sales. This workplace simulation enables students to understand how employees, work-group teams, and departments interact with each other and work together for the goal of the company. (New York City Department of Education, n.d.)

In a sense the entirety of such a learning experience involves Creativity in the sense that the students, as a group, must imagine a business they want to start, research the needs and business opportunities associated with it, and imagine and create an entity that will bring them to life. It is very much a situation in which things are tried, results evaluated, and re-targeting to better address the evolving picture takes place on an ongoing basis.

Business Plans

One central activity to teaching entrepreneurship involves having the students create a business plan. The Biz Kid$ student entrepreneurship website (bizkids.com/themes/entrepreneurship), a rich repository of entrepreneurship education resources based on the Biz Kid$ public television show, offers a number of downloadable tools to support groups of students in doing this. One of these is a guiding template that leads students through the thinking process involved in creating a business plan and asking them important leading questions. Another interesting resource to be found on this website is the "3 Minutes to Change the World" activity, which poses the following learning objectives:

1. Match passions with problems in your community.

2. Utilize ordinary household items in creative ways to solve everyday problems.

3. Turn an idea into action to create sustainable change.

4. Learn how to tell a great story to promote a project.

The Biz Kid$ site also provides links to a great many of the show's original videos, which offer a variety of informative and dramatically presented content on the entrepreneurship theme. These are accompanied by lesson plans and other resources.

Another good source of creativity-oriented entrepreneurship resources and activities is the National Consortium for Entrepreneurship Education's Entrepreneurship Classroom Activities (entre-ed.org/_teach/activits.htm). A few titles include: "Creativity, Innovation, and Problem Solving," "Business Plan Know How," and "Business Startup Simulation".

Elevator Pitches, Commercials, and Trailers

Yet another activity type that joins entrepreneurship with the development and application of creativity skills is the "elevator pitch," a quick-paced, oral presentation to convince investors or others to see the value of a product or service. The elevator pitch involves numerous elements of creativity: imagery, whether it be accomplished by verbal description or real graphics; writing, the choice of words and the sequencing of the ideas they convey; and the use of voice, body language, and the environment to present ideas impactfully. Entrepreneur.com, an online magazine, published an article titled "Watch These Entrepreneurs Pitch Their Start-ups to Judges from Techstars and AlleyNYC." This article offers an explanation and samples of student work on which to model a worthwhile activity. Students will find value in this content, and it is a worthwhile resource. Learn more and see the video at entrepreneur.com/video/250623.

Extending this idea, students can be assigned to create advertisements. Developing video and audio commercials provides a powerful connection between creativity activities and entrepreneurship learning. The Scholastic magazine article "Digital Communication: Student-Designed Commercials" describes several such activities. One notable example is a movie trailer for a book the students have read. Basically, the assignment is, "If this book was made into a movie, what would a commercial promoting that movie look like?" (Vasicek, 2011) Another article, from the Read-WriteThink website titled "Persuasive Techniques in Advertising," lists the following student objectives:

Students will...

- demonstrate an understanding of three persuasive techniques (pathos, logos, and ethos) and other advertising strategies.
- analyze advertisements according to their employment of these techniques.
- demonstrate an understanding of the concept of demographics and specific audience.
- synthesize this knowledge into advertisements of their own creation. (Kuglich, 2016)

The *Forbes* magazine article "How America's Education Model Kills Creativity and Entrepreneurship" opens with this statement: "The current model of education in the United States is stifling the creative soul of our children." (Batten Institute, 2015) While this is troubling for a variety of reasons, it also has significant economic consequences for the future of our country. America has long been unique because of its remarkable ingenuity, innovative capacity, and entrepreneurial spirit. Yet over the last few decades, we have witnessed both a steady decline in the number of startups. An increasing number of studies suggest America's education model fails to promote the kind of creativity, risk-taking, and problem-solving skills necessary for entrepreneurship. This is bad news for a world and labor market that is in the midst of profound transformation. These are very worrisome trends.

The value and promise of the types of activities, resources, and goals highlighted in this section should be apparent. Similarly, the path of entrepreneurship as a way to impact student creativity, along with defining a prime application for it, should resonate for all educators who have their eyes open and the true best interests of our students at heart.

Gaming and Creativity

Video games are a powerful platform from which student creativity can be fostered and developed. Within the reality established by certain varieties of these games, students may experiment in creating things for which meaning, function, and purpose are crucial. Video games provide a canvas on which the products of the imagination of students can be displayed, demonstrated, set in motion, and adopted and used by others. Among other dimensions video games clearly motivate and facilitate student creativity, and do so in ways that require critical thinking, problem solving, innovation, as well as relevance and high levels of accountability of their consistency and functionality. In short, gaming is one of the most effective and engaging contexts in which student creativity can be developed.

In late 2011 Michigan State University announced that an extensive study headed by psychology professor Linda Jackson indicated that boys and girls who play video games tend to be more creative. Professor Jackson offered:

> The MSU findings should motivate game designers to identify the aspects of video game activity that are responsible for the creative effects. Once they do that, video games can be designed to optimize the development of creativity while retaining their entertainment values such that a new generation of video games will blur the distinction between education and entertainment. (Richmond, 2011)

In another research study on the impact of video games on creativity, this one conducted at Penn State, the findings seem to indicate that high arousal, something often associated with students' very strong engagement levels with video games, is a key factor. "When you are highly aroused, the energy itself acts as a catalyst, and the happy mood acts as an encouragement. It is like being in a zone where you cannot be thrown off your game," explain researchers (Avasthi, 2008).

A negative mood, especially when there is low arousal, brings a different kind of energy that makes a person more analytical, which is crucial to creativity as well. "You need defocused attention for being creative," said S. Shyam Sundar, professor of film, video and media studies at Penn State. This is significant, as the proliferation and interest in gaming as a platform for student learning activities continues to increase and gain acceptance.

Minecraft

One video game with tremendous potential in fostering creativity among the students who use it in a variety of ways is Minecraft, a game resource that has garnered wide attention and a devoted following. Minecraft appears to fit the bill as a gaming resource with strong potential to foster creativity in students if implemented in an informed manner with such a goal in mind.

In late January 2016, Anthony Salcito, vice president of Worldwide Education at Microsoft, announced the company's investment in new and expanded editions of Minecraft. Salcito described Minecraft's appeal and impact in the classroom in the following way:

> By creating a virtual world and then advancing in it, students can learn digital citizenship, empathy, social skills and even improve their literacy–while getting real time feedback on their problem solving skills from the teacher. In fact, more than 7,000 classrooms in more than 40 countries around the world are already using Minecraft. (Salcito, 2016)

Minecraft is composed of a complex and rich set of resources, and its likely impact on student learning will extend into a variety of types of learning. Importantly, its emergence and popularity may be the turning point in which schools unabashedly accept the potential that gaming offers to education as they commit to understanding and adopting it. One dimension of this surely will be the way that Minecraft can be used in efforts to foster student creativity. As this is realized, it will further validate and deepen gaming as a genre of student content and as a variety of instructional activity and resource.

There is a great deal about Minecraft, and of course other games that preceded it, that immediately aligns with student creativity. First and foremost the element of play as condition for developing creativity is obviously a defining dimension of participation. Further, collaboration, an element of the specific sort of creativity that today's students will likely need in abundance throughout their lives, is an understood basic element. While in a creative mode, players establish and alter the virtual environment in which their participation takes place. They add and eliminate elements as their needs and imaginations dictate. Further, they can create items, tools, and vehicles with which they succeed or fail at the challenges that take place within the world of Minecraft. Doing so not only involves creative problem solving, as well as free form, imagination-driven creation, but, in a sense, all things created or altered or expanded (creativity) have the strong possibility of being applied to the real world. Or perhaps more accurately, the virtual world in which students play Minecraft.

Minecraft is a creation-rich environment and a wonderful platform for understanding, developing, and applying creativity and reflecting on it. As educators come to understand this, these aspects of Minecraft, as well as programs and curriculum to take advantage of it, will proliferate.

Among its many other dimensions, in Minecraft's Creative Mode, players can build elements of the game themselves, thus the world in which they play, as well as the items that facilitate their play, are created by the players via a simple-to-use interface. In this sense Minecraft becomes a variety of digital art palette.

One of the interesting pieces that clicks with Minecraft is that the very large, extended community of users/players have created and posted a wide variety of YouTube videos that demonstrate and share insights into the dimensions of play. With Minecraft and games that came before and perhaps informed and inspired its creators (e.g., Farmville, and SimCity), we see learners taking control of a game made available to them. In a sense, as players take ownership of the game, become more comfortable and adept at it, and push its boundaries, they are creating the game for themselves—both as individuals and as a community. Still, on a more literal level, another and important approach to the use of gaming as a method for fostering creativity is to establish activities for students in which they create their own games. Even better, if those games are not just for themselves, but for others who comprise their audience, the creativity-inducing aspects of the game will do so more deeply and powerfully.

Student-Created Games

While the classical view of digital games is that they are things to be played another facet to explore and understand is to see gaming as a publishing medium or genre. Games involve characters and action. They are published in the sense that a completed game can be passed on to others who, if it is successful, will be able to access, interpret, and use the game as the author intended.

One good model of how this approach of challenging students to create their own games is provided by the National STEM Video Game Challenge. Details of this multi-year (2011–2015) program remain available at the program's website (stem-challenge.org/stem/#/home), which states:

> Inspired by the Educate to Innovate campaign, President Obama's initiative to promote a renewed focus on Science, Technology, Engineering, and Math (STEM) education, the National STEM Video Game Challenge is a multi-year competition whose goal is to motivate interest in STEM learning among America's youth by tapping into students' natural passion for playing and making video games.

Importantly, the site continues to offer resources needed and commonly used by students to create their own games, including links to digital game production resources (many of them free) such as Gamestar Mechanic, Scratch, Unity, and others. The site also offers game creation instructional content in both print and video form, and teacher guide materials. (E-Line Media & Joan Ganz Cooney Center, 2016)

In essence, student-created games offer students opportunities to teach the subject they've charged themselves to learn about in order to create the game. It's a way to structure an experience for others, their audience. Creating such a game is a learning experience and at once, a cross between being a teacher who informs about a subject and an entertainer who puts on a show. Above all, it's an opportunity for students to create their own universe where they decide how things look, feel, and behave. They create the sort of experience their audience has when they enter it. Another dimension of game creation that supports the development of creativity is that games require writing and speaking and listening skills that are directed at storytelling, the most basic act of creativity.

Resources to Explore Before Getting Started with Gaming

- **Minecraft** (education.minecraft.net)
- **Globaloria** (globaloria.com)
- **PurposeGames** (purposegames.com)
- **Scratch** (scratch.mit.edu)
- **Gamestar Mechanic** (gamestarmechanic.com)
- **GameSalad** (gamesalad.com)
- **GameMaker: Studio** (yoyogames.com/studio)
- **Aris** (arisgames.org)
- **inkle** (inkle.co)
- **Pixel Press** (projectpixelpress.com)
- **Tynker** (tynker.com)

What about the theme of the games? When contemplating engaging students in game creation projects it may be easy to get lost in the impressive variety of powerful digital authoring resources available. These represent opportunities for students to learn a wide variety of skills, everything from narrative writing to visual design to coding. However, it is worthwhile, too, to focus on the theme of the games. What content will the game carry and which format of the game will best communicate that content to the game users, the audience. Taking a step or two back before diving into the experience with students can pay big dividends. Perhaps have students do a little online research to find a game that impresses them, something they can share within a whole group discussion or two about what games are, what they accomplish, and the types of games that will fit in with the other things they are learning and doing currently. This sort of reflection will help focus and direct the high energy unit that is to follow as students actually create a real game to present to a real audience.

A class of students working on creating their own games will likely experience a production environment that, in terms of the educational experiences schools commonly afford students, is uncommon. It will mimic the creative environment currently in place in the real world, whether that workplace be Pixar or a development lab at NASA.

As students develop their games, they might test them on one another throughout the semester. When students have developed their games up to a certain point, the next logical step is to turn to peers and request that they play their game and give them some feedback about what works and what could use more development. Over time, not only do students learn to create games and work with the technology involved, but they also learn how to give and receive feedback that is useful and actionable.

One opportunity to get an idea of the sorts of experiences students have, and the products they create, can be had at the website gallery of Globaloria (globaloria.com/game-gallery/). This site offers an online body of student-created games that can be sorted by student grade level and game theme.

Another highly worthwhile site to investigate when considering making game design part of classroom activities is Gamestar Mechanic (gamestarmechanic.com). This website provides game-based "quests" and courses in game design.

Digital Storytelling

Storytelling is a basic part of the human experience and a highly revered element of our culture. It is closely associated with many of our important institutions, including religion and history. It is not only a rock solid approach to communicating ideas and facts, but the form itself is closely associated with important elements of culture like theater, literature, motion pictures, and television.

Storytelling has long been a part of the broad and varied body of activities that comprise the culture of schooling, although it often has been seen as a sort of extracurricular, enrichment activity. Clearly, it is closely associated with a good many of the skills required in the language arts curriculum: writing and its many component skills, speaking and listening, literature. Further, a storytelling dimension can easily be applied to other subjects, like social studies, in which the fundamental subject component of history can be seen as formalized and accountable storytelling. Storytelling has its place in the science classroom, in which the stories of prominent figures and their contributions to the field are well handled through this approach to communicating information. Today's employers, when focused on the sorts of skills they hope to see in their employees, will often describe communication skills, both written and oral, as being high value skills.

Importantly, creativity is closely associated with storytelling. In fact, it is one area of creativity with which all people likely have some experience. So fundamental to the human functions of communication is the creation of stories that storytelling truly is one of the most basic and natural mechanisms by which creativity is achieved. For educators focusing on student creativity and activities through which it can be developed and applied, storytelling is a natural platform from which this is addressed.

Instructional Practice of Digital Storytelling

With the advent of digital technologies there has been renewed interest in storytelling as technology. It has broadened the type of storytelling possible for the average student. Thus, what has evolved over the past decade or so is the instructional practice of digital storytelling.

Quite simply, digital storytelling is the practice of using digital resources (computers, cameras, camera phones, software, and the like) to tell a story. Used in the classroom, digital technology is an instructional platform from which students and teachers can focus on the craft of storytelling. It is a platform that will not only allow students to work on the very important skill set of writing but will encourage them to engage in a variety of organizational and technology skills, and importantly, focus and reflect on their creative process as they apply it to accomplish a series of highly motivating tasks. Students find digital storytelling to be compelling, because storytelling is something they are already involved and interested in; it is fundamental to the human experience.

What's creative about digital storytelling? All of the elements of writing stories involve the opportunity to present something new: theme, plot, setting, character, and so on. As is often the way digital-age individuals are creative, this may involve adapting already established things and personalizing them in unique ways or recombining existing things in new and novel pairings and relationships. Thus students are not inventing or reinventing the basic elements of storytelling. Rather they are appropriating, making them their own, and putting their own, unique spin on them.

As part of this, web-based research in which students can quickly see what else has been done in telling stories is highly supportive to student exploration as storytellers. This type of research also adds a dimension of authority about what they are working on. Further, as members of a class, students have the opportunity to get and offer feedback on their evolving work as storytellers from peers, engaging in brainstorming, and perfecting their abilities at presenting their stories in a logical and effective sequence and manner. These are skills that will prove increasingly important as they move into higher education and careers.

Finally, students not only exercise and tap their creativity in structuring their story, but in the way they tell it and present it to their audience. Digital storytelling provides a wonderful context, in which students can experiment with and perfect their craft in using technology and media, particularly at the intersection between the two. Today's resources make the creation and use of imagery, sound, movement, and interactivity in even complex projects relatively easy. Using this wide variety of resources comes into focus and becomes meaningful only in context, something that digital storytelling provides naturally and in abundance. With today's technology resources students have the ability, as never before, to opt for any of a great many techniques and effects in their storytelling. They are not, for instance, obliged to choose either drawing, or photo montage, or animated video, or any of a great many other approaches simply because that is what is available, or that is the sole thing they can muster the skill for. Rather, today's user-friendly digital media items are available in such abundance, and offer such deep support for those desiring to express themselves, that student creativity is unleashed and exercised deeply as students focus not on their struggle to make something work passably, but on their ideas and how those ideas impact their world.

Digital Storytelling Resources

There are a wide variety of digital resources available for students and teachers to use in storytelling activities. Many of them are either free or already in their possession as basic items provided with standard technology deployed in schools. Basics, like MS Word and similar word processing programs (OpenOffice, for instance) and PowerPoint and other slide-oriented presentation resources, can be used in numerous ways to support storytelling efforts.

Many resources, like the free, online Storybird (storybird.com) not only can be used for storytelling but provide scaffolding and support that enable students to participate and learn about storytelling as they grow and become better at it. Storybird provides a platform through which users can create sequential stories utilizing a body of artistic images provided by the resource. The students supply plot and verbiage. The availability of imagery without struggle to create or otherwise acquire it enables students to focus on the creative aspects of telling a story. Similarly, use of a resource like this models a process for students who then can follow that model as they eliminate layers of support and take more control of their creative experience.

One of the advantages of a resource like Storybird is that it is not only a platform on which students can create a story easily, focusing on the thinking and languages skills targeted, but it is also a medium for publishing that story, as student stories remain available online. By sending or posting links to the stories, student storytelling work can be disseminated to appropriate audiences, bringing even young students into the world of published authors, a valuable sort of experience not easy to come by before resources of this type were available. Students can also use this platform to collaborate with others on stories.

More useful than knowing about every possible resource would be to understand their types and categories and perhaps, a few notable, "best of breed" examples for each category. In short, there are outline and storyboarding resources, digital comic strip resources, online digital storybook resources, slide format resources, as well as audio and video format resources. And, of course, those are only the principal types. Further, general resources like slide show or presentation resources (e.g., PowerPoint and Prezi) can be used, as can ebook or e-periodical resources like issuu or Youblisher, which allow users to upload content which is then embedded in virtual reality online widgets that simulate the look and feel of the pages of a real book or magazine being turned.

Multimedia authoring tools, like Wixie (wixie.com) and Buncee (buncee.com) can also be great assets for digital storytelling activities. See Part 4: Tools and Resources to Develop Student Creativity in this book for more options. But above all look for examples of projects done by colleagues that resonate as addressing goals and levels of understanding, and let the learning proposition influence the choice of resources and tools for digital storytelling projects.

Beyond resources, communities of similarly interested educators can be invaluable resources in understanding, planning, and implementing digital storytelling activities. ISTE's Digital StoryTelling Network is one very prominent group (connect.iste.org/connect/learningnetworks). Also of note is the StoryKeepers wiki (storykeepers.wikispaces.com).

Digital Storytelling Projects

The curriculum is already rich in ideas and opportunities for digital storytelling to address required learning. Among many other assignments, students might retell a book they read or perhaps adapt its story as they carry the theme forward on their own after analyzing the book. They might retell an historical event (e.g., voyages of discovery, the Chicago fire, the Marco Polo story, and so forth). They might explain how a scientific breakthrough came about (e.g., Edison's lightbulb, Pasteur's discovery, Newton's law of gravity, to name but a few). Apart from this, personal narratives make rich and worthwhile themes for digital storytelling, for example: how I met my best friend, how my parents met, the trip I'd most like to take, and so on.

As is discussed elsewhere in this book, an important dimension to developing student creativity, and providing the guidance and support that students will need as they take on creative projects, has to do with process. A digital storytelling process that supports students will embrace elements of the project process as well as elements of the writing process. While teachers will want to reflect on this and tweak it for their own practice, the following process elements should be considered:

Digital Storytelling Process

Select the theme of the story. Identify the general theme and plot elements and identify the characters and setting (as in all stages in this process, what is done here may be tweaked as the student moves forward). One good way to think of the story is this: the principal character overcomes an obstacle to achieve a goal. The rest of the story elements are there to add flavor and detail to make the story appealing, enjoyable, and believable.

Outlining or storyboarding, which is a specialized form of outlining, are particularly suitable for digital storytelling. In the development stage a finite, manageable (from the point of view of student/class time, effort, level or ability, and so on) number of story elements are created (this could be chapters, scenes, or panels in the case of a comic book, depending on the format chosen). These must introduce and explain who the main character is, where the story is taking place, what the main characters hopes to achieve, what that character must do in order to achieve it, and how and when the goal is achieved. In addition, in the outline phase the sequence that these ideas are shared with the audience is established.

Format. Students or their teachers will need to select a digital format on which to base their digital storytelling projects. Common choices are comic book and graphic novel formats, electronic story book format, slide or presentation format, and video format. There are other formats, and a little reflection on which to choose before beginning a project would be wise as the format chosen will influence the outcome importantly.

Scene definition. Each of the scenes (chapters, panels, and the like) is worked on so that the telling of that element is clear and interesting. This is an ongoing process and likely will be revisited as the story comes together.

Presentation. After reviewing and refining sufficiently, the story is presented to the audience. Based on feedback from the audience the creator may wish to make further modifications before showing it again in a refined version.

When doing digital storytelling projects basic stages like these will likely need to be broken down further in order to manage the process within the parameters of school schedules and classroom spaces.

In her article for The Creative Educator website titled "Six Elements of Good Digital Storytelling: Learn the fundamentals to finding success with digital storytelling," Bernajean Porter, an authority on digital storytelling, offers the following sage advice to ensure success with this instructional approach to developing student creativity. According to Porter, "While there are endless approaches to crafting stories, depending on purpose and audience, at least six elements are considered fundamental to this particular storytelling style." Among the six elements Porter describes are:

Developing Creative Tension—A good story creates intrigue or tension around a situation that is posed at the beginning of the story and resolved at the end, sometimes with an unexpected twist. The tension of an unresolved or curious situation engages and holds the viewer until reaching a memorable end.

Showing Not Telling—Unlike traditional oral or written stories, images, sound, and music can be used to show a part of the context, create setting, give story information, and provide emotional meaning not provided by words. Both words and media need to be revealed through details rather than be named or simply stated.

Developing Craftsmanship—A good story incorporates technology in artful ways, demonstrating craftsmanship in communicating with images, sound, voice, color, white space, animations, design, transitions, and special effects. Ask yourself whether your media resources are decorating, illustrating, or illuminating.

(Porter, 2015)

Events-Based Activities

One way of adding a special value and quality to activities designed to develop student creativity is through the staging of events for that purpose. This also has the effect of supporting students in their participation in such activities by providing an authentic context for them. An important dimension of this is that these events organize and provide an audience for student work. Such events add a level of excitement and anticipation to student learning activities. They also provide built-in opportunities to acknowledge students for their hard work and creativity. Members of the larger learning community, both within and beyond the limits of the school, can be invited to share in and learn from the experience.

Examples

There are many events that highlight and celebrate student creativity and innovations. However, there is little certainty that one will be available precisely when needed or that it will perfectly fit a given instructional effort. Far better to view the examples described here as models on which you and others in your school community can base your own events.

FIRST LEGO LEAGUE ANNUAL CHALLENGE

A good, instructive example of this type of event, one that is held every year, both on a local level and a national one, is the First Lego League annual challenge (www.firstlegoleague.org/challenge). In this event, or more accurately, series of related events that sequentially build on one another, student robotics teams respond to a uniform challenge. The challenge is a social/technical "real-world" problem for which the team must design a robot that will cope with the problem, by dint of its design, construction, and programming.

Student teams compete with one another by putting in their robot's best performance and receiving points from judges. The design team with the highest score wins. Robots in this event are constructed from the Lego variety of student robotics materials. These materials are priced to be within reach for public schools and require no more expertise than the skills and understandings that students and teacher coaches acquire by using them as they participate.

It is common for these events to draw press coverage and for school communities to acknowledge participants and their entries and efforts with celebrations on their own. Photos and videos taken and uploaded to a variety of online sharing resources document and celebrate the creative efforts of these students. It is also common for students to document their own Lego robot creations on their own through video that they share online. In this way, one form of student creativity naturally lends itself to others that involve other formats and efforts.

LEGO SMART CREATIVITY CONTEST

Another Lego event, this contest challenges teachers and their classes to, "create a video, no longer than 150 seconds in length, which showcases how you use Lego Education solutions to spark student innovation." The contest's online FAQ sheet further states: "Contestants are encouraged to think beyond the books and focus on the power of the Lego brick! Maybe your entry will feature students writing and performing a skit or perhaps you would like to sing an original song! You could even create a Lego brick animation!" (https://c10645061.ssl.cf2.rackcdn.com/misc/legosmartcontestfaq.pdf)

Figure 10.3 Students competing with their robots in the First Lego League challenge.

The contest overtly is described as one for teachers. But an examination of the winning videos linked on the event's website reveals that it is very much a demonstration of how students respond to creative challenges and prompts their teachers provides them. What results is very much a partnership between teachers and their students.

INVENTION CONVENTION

A good example of how the event idea can be implemented on a much more local level is provided by a 2013 news article from the *Gadsden Times*. The article describes an afterschool enrichment program in Gadsden City, Alabama. Schools there held an Invention Convention contest, judged by local business leaders, and awarded prizes and gave acknowledgement to students who came up with inventions that addressed real-world problems or needs. Many students made inventions to solve or prevent problems in their own lives. For example,

- Fifth-grader Jackson Skelton suffered a head injury one summer while kneeboarding, so he made a four-layer helmet for use during water sports.

- Julendria Nowell from Mitchell Elementary made a utensil sorter to make doing dishes after dinner more fun and easier.

- Third-grader Rueben Gaspar has to deal with his mother always telling him to put away his game system. So he built, finished, and painted a wood center that would allow him to play his games without the need to put them away.

- Other students invented things to help those close to them.

- Takiyah Thomas from Thompson Elementary made a massaging shirt because her mother has a bad back.

- Fourth-grader Bradley Sparks from Eura Brown made a model for a solar-powered, voice-activated wheelchair with text messaging capability, because his mother has mobility problems and he wanted to make things easier for her.

(Davidson, 2013)

The website (inventionconvention.org), while intended for Ohio students, bears information and guidance on how schools and other local organizations can host and participate in an event by summing up the process it hopes to involve students in. The Invention Convention provides free curriculum and hosts regional competitions throughout the state. It is aligned with Ohio's New Learning Standard and its curriculum focuses on the following sequential process:

1. Identifying a problem

2. Problem-solving and critical-thinking processes to solve the problem

3. Developing the invention idea and designing a prototype of the solutions

The Invention Convention is not a science fair, but a STEAM-feeder program designed to expose students in grades K–8 to multiple problem-solving methods, which both hones the real-life skills of students and increases their interest in STEAM-related careers (inventionconvention.org, 2016).

THE PARADIGM CHALLENGE

A newer competition is The Paradigm Challenge (projectparadigm.org). The competition's website describes it as an "annual competition that inspires youth innovation to address important social issues. The first annual Challenge generated new ideas to prevent injuries and fatalities from home fires—America's #1 disaster threat."

Interestingly, student submissions are simply governed by the following statement: "What types of entries are accepted? We welcome all ideas, including posters, videos, inventions, messages, community events, websites, mobile apps, or anything else that will help save lives."

The event's website offers a short video that explains the methods and goals of the program, outlining the challenge and inviting students to participate. It opens with the statement "let's learn how to change the world" and offers the "Six Steps to Solve Any Challenge," which is a process by which students can understand important problems and come up with solutions to them. It uses finding homes for stray animals as an example and model. These include:

- Step One—Study the Problem
- Step Two—Observe What Others Are Doing
- Step Three—List All Imaginable Ideas
- Step Four—Visualize Each Idea
- Step Five—Engage Others for Further Input on the Most Promising Ideas
- Step Six—Decide Which Idea Is Best

The video concludes with the statement: "With these six steps you can solve any challenge. Are you ready to change the world?" (ProjectParadigm.org, 2016)

The approach demonstrated by The Paradigm Challenge is conceived to embrace a wide variety of types of challenges with a uniform methodology and format. As such, this event offers a good model for schools interested in establishing their own challenge.

RUBE GOLDBERG, INC.

The Rube Goldberg organization (rubegoldberg.org) is a group dedicated to preserving and celebrating the work of Rube Goldberg, a Pulitzer Prize winning cartoonist who was well known for his extremely fanciful cartoons of crazy and excessive inventions. The organization also supports an annual contest in which students are invited to create their own "fanciful machines in the spirit of those conceived by Rube, himself."

Both on the website and elsewhere there are wonderful videos to be found of contestants' submissions to these contests. A few examples:

Andrew's 8th Grade Rube Goldberg Project—Final:
youtube.com/watch?v=3jQXN8SMewo

Rube Goldberg Machine made by kids: youtube.com/watch?v=WouOdkM_QBE

Mrs. Corron's Physical Science 2011 Rube Goldberg Projects:
youtube.com/watch?v=1r-Q2wlimJ0

Lego great ball contraption Rube Goldberg machine—BrickFair Virginia 2014:
youtube.com/watch?v=u_dADLKJ5i8

Power of Optics: A light-powered Rube Goldberg machine: tinyurl.com/gm54xg4

For those interested in building Rube Goldberg Machines, another recommended resource is "Build Your Own Rube Goldberg Machine," an illustrated text available free online at: tinyurl.com/hjlapjk

ODYSSEY OF THE MIND

Odyssey of the Mind (odysseyofthemind.com) is an international educational program that provides creative problem-solving opportunities for students from kindergarten through college. Problems ranging from building mechanical devices to presenting their own interpretation of literary classics are solved by teams who bring their solutions to competition on the local, state, and world level.

There was a time when schools everywhere held science fairs, some of which highlighted truly creative submissions from students. The science fair is no longer a staple of school culture and life, and in places where it persists, it often highlights student work that amounts to little more than traditional student research reports that are presented on trifold poster boards. Often there are few truly creative submissions coaxed from students.

The Odyssey of the Mind website notes that challenges presented to students "are designed for competition, with scoring components and limitations, or rules to be followed. The long-term problems change every year. They fall into five general categories. These are mechanical/vehicle, technical performance, classics, structure and performance."

For the mechanical/vehicle problems, "teams design, build and operate vehicles of various sizes and with various power sources." In the area of classics, students handle a problem that is "based on the classical—from literature to architecture to art." Performance problems involve teams of students who present "performances that revolve around a specific theme and incorporate required elements." Structure problems involve students in designing and building structures, using only balsa wood and glue. Technical performance problems require students to make innovative contraptions and incorporate artistic elements into their solutions.

The Odyssey of the Mind website offers a body of resources, including problem descriptions, practice problems, and classroom activities. It also provides important links and contacts for those interested in participating. Students at all levels of schooling K–12 are eligible to participate in their own age category. The event is popular in the United States and a number of other nations around the world.

More Resources

A few other student creativity events worth noting and studying as you formulate a model for an event of your own include the following challenges and competitions.

ADOBE YOUTH VOICES (AYV)

AYV is the Adobe Foundation's signature global initiative to increase creativity in education, which is critical to improving the lives of young people today and well into the future. This program encourages youth 13 to 19 years of age to create original media works on issues like relationships, human rights, and the environment. Since 2006, more than 190,000 youth from 60 countries have participated in AYV programs developing skills central to creative confidence (Adobe Systems Incorporated, 2016).

Maker-Based Learning

Kids naturally want to explore their world. They want to discover how it works and what they can make and do. They love to experiment with things, combining parts and pieces they find. In other words they love to tinker. And kids naturally learn by tinkering. One archetypal example of this can be seen in the Hole-in-the-Wall project, a now, near-famous anecdote in which Sugata Mitra, an Indian computer scientist, set up a computer in a New Delhi marketplace frequented by unsupervised kids. Mitra set up a computer there so that the kids would have access to its screen display and touchpad interface through a hole in the wall. Those children, by the way, received only a poor level of education and had absolutely no experience using computers. It turned out that the children found the computer and after considerable tinkering with it, figured out how to use it and taught one another. The project seems to indicate that for some important learning outcomes, formal education isn't necessary, that is if students can tinker. Mitra, by the way, repeated this experiment in other locations in India with much the same results. Mitra recounts this experiment and its results in full in his Ted Talk YouTube video titled "Sugata Mitra: Can kids teach themselves?" (tinyurl.com/pzbfbx6)

More recently, a similar experience was recounted in the Wired Magazine article "Going Global? The Growing Movement to Let Kids Learn Just by Tinkering" (wired. com/2014/10/pencils-of-promise). In this instance, Leslie Young, at a schoolhouse in rural Agorhome, Ghana, gave access to tablet computers to a class of 5th graders. None of these students had any experience with computers. The outcome was similar to Mitra's in India. After a while the students figured out how to use the device to browse the web (Lapowsky, 2014).

Tinkering is a powerful approach to learning. According to the Nation of Makers page on the White House website: (www.whitehouse.gov/nation-of-makers):

> America has always been a nation of tinkerers, inventors, and entrepreneurs. In recent years, a growing number of Americans have gained access to technologies such as 3D printers, laser cutters, easy-to-use design software, and desktop machine tools. This, in combination with freely available information about how to use, modify, and build upon these technologies and the availability of crowd funding platforms, is enabling more Americans to design and build almost anything. ... Empowering students and adults to create, innovate, tinker, and make their ideas and solutions into reality is at the heart of the Maker Movement. Since the first-ever White House Maker Faire, the White House has continued to support opportunities for students to learn about STEM through making, expand the resources available for maker entrepreneurs, and foster the development of advanced manufacturing in the U.S.

This statement illustrates how thoroughly maker culture has established itself as a trend for U.S. society. Many see it as a positive force in developing and ensuring the presence of creative individuals. The Whitehouse.gov site offers a good deal of insight and information about the maker movement and the sorts of activities, projects, and products associated with it.

Tinkering with things is a very natural, informal, but powerful way that people learn about how things work in their world. It's also an approach through which their natural capacity for creativity is sparked, developed, and applied to both the fancies of their imagination and to real-world problems. We find a very strong case for the legitimacy of this approach in literature on instructional approaches like active learning, hands-on learning, and constructionism.

Even though the dominant forms and bodies of knowledge in education currently favor standards and research-based direct instructional approaches to teaching and learning, maker-based learning is well supported by established theory, including the related theories of constructivist and constructionist learning. Constructionism is a theory/philosophy that is inspired, informed, and built on the more well-known field of constructivist learning. In constructionism, a philosophy of learning championed by Seymour Papert and colleagues several decades ago at MIT, learners build knowledge and structures of understanding as they build structures in the real world. Further, some instructional theorists see constructionist learning as aligned with flow state or optimal experience–oriented learning opportunities, which are conditions that foster creativity.

Making, that is creating things through a process that includes imagining, tinkering/experimenting, constructing, refining, and testing, can include a very wide variety of activities, crafts, processes, and technologies. It can include everything from robotics and computerized fabrication to woodworking and baking. In the context of school instructional programs it may take the place it formerly held just a few decades back by wood and metal working, and ceramics shops. These subjects were closely associated with an industrial arts component of the educational program, something now out of favor and which was replaced in a great many schools and districts by computer labs and general, basic computer use classes. It is worth noting that the latter is now often replaced by the presence of laptops and tablets in subject area classrooms (with the exception of specialized computing courses like business computing, digital drafting and design, and audio and video classes). Makerspaces or makerclasses may be a natural successor to the industrial arts programs the past. However, the industrial arts classes of bygone decades were often conceived as providing an introductory experience to a possible career path for those students not necessarily headed to college. Maker-based learning, by contrast, often directly involves skills that are found in STEM curiculum, which represents and important segment of the core of academic learning. For instance: understanding the nature of direct current circuitry to add lights to a project (science), programming an Arduino processor to direct a simple robot (technology), building an electromagnet to move objects across a surface (engineering), and calculating the area of a plane to determine the amount of material needed to cover a structure (math). Such projects often feature the use of technology as part of the experimenting, construction, and documentation of what's achieved in the makerspace.

142

Makerspace Essentials

A few common and recommended items and activity types to include in your makerspace are listed here.

Student designed, constructed, and programmed robots. Lego robotics materials are the most popular variety for this type of instructional application. This type of resource can support students in conceiving, constructing, programming, and running their own robot inventions. Much of this involves making by tinkering as students create their own robot ideas and make those robots work (see the ISTE book, *Getting Started with Lego Robotics*).

Roger Wagner's HyperDuino, along with other items like Makey Makey. These activity types allow students to establish an interface between the real world and the computer through simple cable connections. Students using these items can make a wired connection from their computer to a real world object, be it 2D or 3D, gather resulting signals, and process those signals with software resulting in purposes, applications, and inventions only limited by their imaginations.

3D printers. This relatively low cost variety of material bridges the realms of real world objects and digital technology. Students communicate digitally with these machines, directing the printer to produce the 3D items. Ideas are "concretized" through this approach, which in turn lends inspiration, purpose, and application to creativity.

LittleBits and other electronics kits. These items feature circuits, sensors, switches, LED lights, and on and on. A wide variety of things that involve contemporary uses of electronics can be created using DIY electronics components that come in convenient kits suitable for classrooms. Using this approach students can bring to life ideas they imagine. Students can learn how to use and apply these types of components and, more important, base new ideas on them as they create.

Wearable Technology. Electronic jewelry, simple mobile sensors and recording devices worn on belts or clipped to pockets, headlamps, and more, are examples of wearable technology. Real-world maker projects in this area are practical for classrooms and appealing to students. Such items can be constructed from individually purchased components or taken from kits acquired for other purposes (like Lego Robotics and LittleBits kits). However, there are some items on the market, like the HelloWorld kit, specifically directed at wearable technology for kids.

Arduino, Raspberry Pi, and similar low cost computing processors. Arduino (arduino.cc/) and Raspberry Pi (raspberrypi.org/) mini processors/controllers (and others like the MSP430 LaunchPad and the Teensy 2.0) are inexpensive, light, small scale (Raspberry Pi is the size of a credit card), programmable and can do the simple processing needed for basic student projects (e.g. cause a series of lights, move simple robots, set up a motion sensor, etc.) They can connect with peripherals like a keyboard or monitor or TV. They can run numerous programming resources suitable for students like MIT's free **Scratch** (scratch.mit.edu).

Other technology-based areas can augment, supplement, and complement the aforementioned items and activities. They include:

Digital still and video photography, audio recording and production. These activities enable the documentation and sharing of 3D projects.

Stop motion animation/clay animation. These activities involve the creation of models to be photographed and incorporated into the full video. Tech4Learning's Frames software (tech4learning.com/frames/) is well suited for this sort of creative project.

Kinetic sculpture. This particular type of project involves the incorporation of electronic components. BirdBrain Technologies' Hummingbird Robotics Kit (hummingbirdkit.com) is directed at this sort of activity.

The impressive and enticing materials and resources in a makerspace will not, in and of themselves, impact student creativity. Resources, particularly those acquired as kits, often come with instructions for prescribed projects. These are recipe- or template-driven "projects" for students to do using the resources. While these may be useful for instructing students in how to use the resources, they generally do not elicit or develop student creativity. As noted elsewhere in this book, student creativity comes from the open-ended challenge to produce something, often for a purpose.

About the makerspace, itself: a makerspace is part physical setting and part conceptual construct. It is a collection of resources and attitudes about doing and learning, often in a way that is social. Collaborative learning is stressed. That is, students learn from one another and support one another, with a teacher or other resident expert sometimes available for guidance. The stress also is on learning through doing, experimenting, and experience. Makerspaces need not necessarily involve extravagant, permanent use of space or very expensive materials. Resources like 3D printers or robotics kits can be shared, computers used may be those used for other purposes by a class when not involved in maker activities. The focus of a makerspace should be on the activities and possibilities that student learners are empowered to engage in, meaning that the makerspace itself need not be a technology showplace.

While a makerspace can be a classroom or a portion of one, there's more to a makerspace than the physical space. Student behavior is likely to be markedly different in a makerspace, even for students who remain productive and on-task. Learning there is informal and motivated by fun and self-fulfillment. Makerspaces are inherently social. Students will want and need to gather in small groups to work on things and move about to see and learn from what others are doing. It may prove to be a space that draws more outside visitors than an ordinary classroom, as students may want to invite in experts and other adults for support.

A fine extension to a makerspace, and making activities in general, would be a class blog or website. Such a publication would provide students an opportunity to report about their experiments, both successes and failures, to the world outside the classroom. It is a platform that accommodates student writing, photos, scans, drawings and other graphics, and audio and video files. The blog can even embed a player widget. (Although the sound file itself will need to be hosted at resource setup for that specific purpose—SoundCloud can be used for audio; YouTube for video.) The blog would not only give students a platform on which they can document and archive their work, but using the Comments function it can be used to elicit and record feedback from interested audience members.

Genius Hour, 20% Time, and Tinker Time

In order to develop their creativity, students must be given time in which to be creative. However, considering that making creativity a goal of instruction is, in and of itself, a departure from the predominant approach to teaching and learning in place in many schools today, it follows that the organizational structures, as well as the goal of creativity, are not part of the current body of practice with which educators are familiar and comfortable.

A few ideas to address this need have emerged over the past few years. Certainly it has attracted the attention of a large group of teachers. Much has been made of the well-publicized institution of 20% Time (also simply 20 Time), which is attributed to the culture of Google, and 3M before it. The idea is that employees, while on the clock and formally being compensated for their time, are given 20% of their workweek with which to explore ideas on their own, independent of the assignments for which they are held accountable. The general understanding understanding is that this freedom to spend some time following their own curiosity and passion results in innovation, in creative ideas that ultimately satisfy the inner drive and intellectual needs of today's students as they develop numerous skill sets, including those need to assume the roles of problem solvers and solution generators.

In a significant number of schools, teachers have begun implementing variations on this free-use approach to the use of time, calling their program 20% Time, Tinker Time, Genius Hour, or something similar. While educators may understand that granting freedom to students will necessarily require all involved to conform to a particular set of ideas about responsibility and accountability, it is also useful to understand that this is not the same thing as granting students unstructured "free time." Unstructured free time for which there is no expectations, particularly no expectations concerning student learning and personal growth, is not 20% Time.

One issue to define early on is whether or not students are being granted time and freedom to explore ideas and projects in general, or if their exploration efforts are clearly directed at things that relate to the overall body of learning of the subject and class they receive that time and freedom in. In relation to this, it may be effective to have students submit a written agreement about what they will work on, one in which they personally define its relationship to the overarching work and goals of the class (perhaps defined by the teacher or by the class as an effort led by the teacher), and further agreeing to modify this in writing as their explorations and needs dictate.

Simple accountability measures like keeping a learning/activity journal for their 20% Time and agreeing to make presentations to the extended learning community of the class periodically on what they've done, accomplished, or produced, may prove effective in supporting actual student learning. While such periodic presentations don't have to result in grades, a rubric designed to give the students some feedback on how well they've invested their time and effort can be supportive in helping students understand their performance in an area that is rarely reviewed, let alone even offered, in our schools.

One source of clarity on this topic is the online resource 20 Time in Education (20timeineducation.com). It offers explanations about the history of this type of practice, some guidance in structured variations of ways to implement it (e.g., 20 Time, Genius Hour), and includes links to other worthwhile resources like Joy Kirr's 20% Time/Genius Hour Live Binder (www.livebinders.com/play/play/829279).

In keeping with the goal of developing creativity, it would be most valuable for students to identify their own areas of focus and effort concerning activities to be engaged in using 20% Time. Still, the following list provides some ideas about the sorts of activities that may work well in this context:

How to Use 20% Time in the Classroom

- Write a book, nonfiction or fiction—do it as a graphic novel or an ebook to be posted online. Instead of the book, perhaps write a series of articles that eventually can be aggregated into a collection that can form a book.

- Start and update a blog that documents and publishes findings and thoughts on a theme in the news or a subject of interest.

- Create a how-to tutorial item—perhaps as a video to be posted or as a text item shared online at a document-sharing resource.

- Write up recipes, food or other products. Aggregate these into a book.

- Create a movie by writing a script, then filming and editing.

- Raise money for a cause you care about—research and identify a cause that relates to the subject of the course and class.

- Curate a list of resources relating to a theme of interest, hopefully one that relates to the themes of the course and class—list names, give explanatory annotations, and rate items included by a rating system you devise.

- Research the back stories of items in the news that relate to a theme. Write up the results as a magazine article or blog post.

- Research opportunities for a given class theme—locate contacts and engage in e-correspondence with luminaries, notable people, and experts in a given area that relates to a theme being studied.

- Establish and maintain a digital scrapbook of images and captions of items relating to a theme of interest.

In implementing 20% Time and affording students the freedom to tinker and create, to follow their curiosity and their intellectual passions, teachers may realize a number of instructional goals as they implement a variety of instructional approaches.

There is a good deal of common ground between the 20% Time and project-based learning (PBL). Indeed, PBL is very consistent with the idea of allowing students to select their own learning focus, to identify their own approaches to investigating it, and to define their own way of communicating and demonstrating what at they've learned. Progress in PBL projects is often marked by self-management in terms of time allocation.

Twenty Percent Time is a structure that provides freedom and time, but it also requires activity to fill the space established by them. In this way, it addresses the related goal of giving students voice and choice in their learning. When afforded 20% Time, students need something to work on if that time is to represent something meaningful and worthwhile in their educational experience. Whatever the method of instruction, whether it be project-based learning or traditional teacher-led direct instruction, a dimension of voice and choice will enrich it, making for deeper, more meaningful learning. There is a confluence, therefore; when giving students voice and choice and affording them 20% Time, they are provided mutually supporting benefits.

20% TIME AND STANDARDS

It is worth noting that 20% Time allows for students to engage in activities that address important educational standards. And so, including it in instructional planning is done on firm ground.

Among the Common Core State Standards addressed are:

- Draw on information from multiple print or digital sources, demonstrating the ability to locate an answer to a question quickly or to solve a problem efficiently (CCSS.ELA-LITERACY.RI.7).

- Respond to questions and suggestions from peers and add details to strengthen writing as needed (CCSS.ELA-LITERACY.W.5).

- Use technology, including the Internet, to produce and publish writing and to interact and collaborate with others (CCSS.ELA-LITERACY.W.6).

- Gather relevant information from multiple print and digital sources, assess the credibility and accuracy of each source, and integrate the information while avoiding plagiarism (CCSS.ELA-LITERACY.CCRA.W.8).

The ISTE Standards for Students also emphasize student voice and expression, through such indicators as:

6.c. communicate complex ideas clearly and effectively by creating or using a variety of digital objects such as visualizations, models or simulations.

7.b. use collaborative technologies to work with others, including peers, experts or community members, to examine issues and problems from multiple viewpoints.

The Next Generation Science Standards lists eight types of Performance Expectations, behaviors associated with required Science Learning. Among these are: Developing and Using Models, Planning and Carrying Out Investigations, Constructing

Explanations and Designing Solutions, and Obtaining, Evaluating, and Communicating Information.

Motivation, Interest, Passion, and Spark

If anything can be described as the Holy Grail of instruction, it is motivation. Teachers understand that motivation is the lubricant that moves instruction along the path to success. How to achieve motivation, though, is elusive. Many come to understand that intrinsic motivation, that is, a force that engages and moves students to participate not through the promise of extraneous punishments and rewards but through the promise of the activity itself, is the key to successful planning and implementation of instruction.

There is an important relationship between creativity and motivation. In essence, students who are engaged in creative efforts are necessarily highly motivated. They have such a vested interest in the result of that effort that motivation follows strongly. In that sense, when teaching a body of content by engaging students in the creation of a product or performance that relates to it, student motivation is ensured as they research that theme, reflect on—analyze—and draw conclusions about, and express and communicate their learning and conclusions on that theme.

Associated with the sort of motivation that accompanies creative effort is the idea of student passion, and along with that, students' personal spark. *Atlantic Magazine* reports Alexandra Usher, one of the authors of the 2012 Center on Educational Policy report "Student Motivation: An Overlooked Piece of School Reform," as saying, "Not surprisingly, if students see a direct connection between what they are learning and their own interests and goals, they are likely to be more motivated." (Richmond, 2012)

There's a strong connection here. When students are tasked to identify a subject to investigate, they are likely to choose something that they find personally interesting, something that personally resonates for them (choice). Further, when the focus of this work is personally interesting students are not only motivated to learn about it but are highly motivated to communicate about their interest in it, what they have learned about it, as well as their opinions on the subject (voice). In other words the conditions for being creative, as well as the energy for it, are present. There is a relationship between personal interest and creative efforts.

In her article "Ideas to help students find their passion in learning," youth-development consultant and author Susan Ragsdale writes, "A 'spark' is the inner light that gives us energy, motivation, purpose, and focus. It makes us feel alive when we're doing what we love. Sparks are expressed as talents, qualities, or passions. And when we operate from our sparks, we shine and offer something good, beautiful, and useful to the world." To illustrate, she relates a number of instances when her own teachers assigned her creative projects that helped develop her sparks and find her passion. (Ragsdale, 2014)

To many, the idea that schools may not be providing an education that addresses these issues and results in this sort of learning may seem unsettling. At the very least, asking ourselves whether or not this is the case would be important time and effort well spent.

It may be the case that students need support in identifying and confidently communicating precisely what it is that they are passionate about in life, as well as in learning. Teachers can have students reflect on the things they gravitate toward, the things they do online, the news items that attract their attention, the games they find appealing, the entertainers who most interest them, and so on. Drawing up lists and then annotating list items with short descriptions and reflective comments about why these things appeal to them and what they mean to them may seem to the students as coming totally out of the blue, having little precedent in things they've ever done in school previously. Still, launching students on the path of self-discovery, particularly as preparation for and as part of reflective understanding after the fact of activities that develop and apply their creativity, will add a good deal of value.

Student creative work is a platform through which students can discover, indulge, and develop a degree of mastery in their areas of interest and passion. This is important preparation for their future. Further, activities that develop creativity as a result of working in their area of passion establish strong motivation for learning, something that can be applied to and impact other dimensions of learning.

STEAM and Creativity

"Art and music require the use of both schematic and procedural knowledge and, therefore, amplify a child's understanding of self and the world," Dr. Jerome Kagan, eminent psychologist and emeritus professor at Harvard University, said at the Johns Hopkins Learning, Arts, and the Brain summit in 2009. With this theoretical foundation in mind, educators are experimenting with merging art and science lessons.

There are a variety of things needed in order for our schools to effectively make developing creativity an achievable goal. We are not likely to find our schools offering creativity classes, nor would doing so necessarily result in an ideal or effective way to assure that our schools graduate students who are knowledgeable in and adept at creativity. What's needed, therefore, is a clear understanding and model of where in the general instructional program creativity can be placed and done. If not as a separate subject or scheduled class, then where within the current organizational model can we establish an effective context for fostering creativity? One answer to this crucial question is STEAM programs, that through careful planning the Arts can be supported as an essential facet of instruction and that one contribution they can make to fostering creativity is as a natural approach to further establishing and deepening the creative dimension of the STEM subjects of science, technology, engineering, and math.

In the 2012 *Scientific American* magazine article titled "From STEM to STEAM: Science and Art Go Hand-in-Hand," author Steven Ross Pomeroy says that "there is a growing group of advocates who believe that STEM is missing a key component—one that is equally deserved of renewed attention, enthusiasm, and funding. That component is the arts. If these advocates have their way, STEM would become STEAM." While it is far from the only possible avenue to explore in introducing and focusing on creativity in the area of STEM learning it is a very promising one that will have the added effect of supporting the presence of the arts in our schools, a body instructional subjects that will offer value in fostering creativity beyond their role in the STEM subjects, too. (Pomeroy, 2012)

In a strong sense, a school that has math, science, and technology instructional programs but that keeps these subject classes separate and discreet doesn't truly have a STEM program. A true STEM program not only implies and requires the inclusion of these subject areas, but it requires that they be taught and learned in an integrated fashion, not as separate entities that individually comprise isolated elements of effort and learning. There are important connections that cross the boundaries among these areas and that unify them. Understanding the contexts in which they are related and connected is an essential element of a STEM program, without which it cannot truly be stated that they jell into what we aspire to be the crucial area of learning we call STEM.

What's needed to pull these areas of learning together meaningfully often is another element or structure, a platform that unites them all, something greater than the individual parts, something that gives additional meaning and purpose.

One such platform is the area of projects, while another is the arts. It should come as little surprise that these two areas are related. Adding these results in the freshly conceived area of study called STEAM. We arrive at this new acronym by the addition of the "A" (for arts) which, among other things, can function as a sort of adhesive through which the various elements of a STEM project can be held together.

The arts offer great learning advantages, both in the area of developing creativity and in the area of fostering learning in the various STEM constituent instructional elements. STEAM enables students to demonstrate what they've learned in the STEM content areas.

A time lapse animated video that illustrates how seed germinates, becomes a plant, matures, bears fruit, which then is eaten by an animal that passes its seeds to begin the cycle again, would be a worthwhile example of STEAM in action. A student engaged in a learning project would do research to learn the basic idea and find useful examples—he might mine the web for images to use in his product—and would use a variety of digital resources to create, publish, and share the finished product. Thus, this student would move from online research (technology) to the biology of plant reproduction (science) to doing a photo collage or series of drawings (visual art) to illustrate and communicate his learning, to using an animation program that involves simple programming (engineering) to create the final product. The process would also likely include using language, reading the research content, writing captions for photos, and narrating the explanation of the animation (literacy). In designing the illustrations and the timing of their appearance in the video the student would likely employ counting, measuring, and a number calculations (math). During the course of doing the project, all areas of STEAM would be touched on.

Involving students in learning across the curriculum is a goal that is worth pursuing. But it is not always something that is practical or within reach. Considering the organizational approach currently adhered to in our schools, one that continues to have students attend classes that reflect the identity of just one of the STEM continuum of subjects at a time, the principal or driving content focus of a lesson (like the life science lesson just described) is something that can be determined by the teacher of the STEM area subject class in which the assignment is given. The arts dimension execution of the project can be handled with support from an arts teacher if one is available, or handled by self-supporting students who take advantage of technology. That being said, achieving an arts dimension can be a simple matter of including a reflective component to these projects. In some cases, students might be asked to reflect on and identify other areas of learning that are involved in their projects. As well, they might be directed to investigate these areas, either to a small degree or as another project entirely. They might even touch base with the other teachers for a degree of support.

In her Edutopia blog post titled "Creativity is the Secret Sauce in STEM," Science evangelist Ainissa Ramirez states, "Creativity is the secret sauce to science, technology, engineering, and math (STEM). It is a STEM virtue. While most scientists and engineers might be reluctant to admit that, and to accept the concept of STEAM (where A is for Art), I've witnessed that the best of the best are the most creative."

She goes on to explain how in teaching she sees the artistic approach of "the metaphor" as being a prime way to teach science, and how in using it she accomplishes effective teaching in the area of chemistry. This is something of particular note as the class in question consisted of liberal arts students, many of whom had long avoided making science something they took seriously (Ramirez, 2013).

Get Started with STEAM

For a quick snapshot of some other STEAM projects, take a look at the following videos and articles.

- **STEAM projects 2014:** youtube.com/watch?v=HRQwYiBKo0M

- **STEM to STEAM:** stemtosteam.org/about

- **STEM vs. STEAM: Why the "A" Makes a Difference:** edudemic.com/stem-vs-steam-why-the-a-makes-all-the-difference/

- **STEAM Ahead: Merging Arts and Science Education:** pbs.org/newshour/rundown/the-movement-to-put-arts-into-stem-education

- **Putting Art in STEM:** nytimes.com/2014/11/02/education/edlife/putting-art-in-stem.html?_r=0

- **S.T.E.A.M Science Technology Engineering Arts and Math:** youtube.com/watch?v=qdD69KV59wo

- **Growing from STEM to STEAM—Tips to team up the arts and sciences in your classroom:** tinyurl.com/z5rh2l9

Chapter 11

Learning Activities to Develop Student Creativity

It's worthwhile to view activities designed to develop student creativity in reference to Bloom's taxonomy. It is a widely accepted conceptual framework that functions as the backbone of numerous teaching philosophies in current favor, particularly those that stress the value of skills over pure content. Bloom's taxonomy most commonly refers to the portion of the work done by the group headed up by Benjamin Bloom. It was published in 1956, associated with the cognitive domain of learning. While it has been interpreted, adapted, and updated consistently since it was first published, generally it is depicted as a pyramid or other hierarchy, the upper levels of which identify the "higher order thinking (and learning) skills," which represent valued learning goals for many educators. They are listed as follows:

- Creating
- Evaluating
- Analyzing
- Applying
- Understanding
- Remembering (and acquiring factual content)

In viewing Bloom's taxonomy we see creativity as an essential element of the whole of learning, and one that is considered an indication of having achieved a level of sophisticated and highly competent learning. It is important to bear in mind, though, that this depiction is not that of a map that plots a sequential path to learning that involves first remembering, then understanding, and so on as one slowly and surely climbs the various levels and types of activities that support and manifest them. In a well-designed activity or project, as is true in a well-designed and implemented program of general instruction and learning that is directed at involving students in developing creativity, it is almost a certainty that all levels depicted in the taxonomy will be addressed, engaged, and contribute to the overall experience. It is useful to bear this in mind should doubts present themselves that by pursuing creativity, other aspects of learning, particularly those sometimes considered more practical, will be slighted or overlooked. Similarly, it is important for us to bear in mind that none of these levels can or should practically be pursued in isolation and that all should be considered as part of a whole, wherein the elements support one another.

It is also worthwhile for us to be aware that Bloom's taxonomy represents only a portion of a broader conceptual framework associated with the work of Bloom's group, although it is very commonly known as the whole of it. In addition to the aforementioned representation of learning in the cognitive domain, there is also a framework for learning in the affective domain, a domain that if it were much utilized might be closely associated with developing student creativity. Further, there is a psychomotor kinesthetic domain of learning, as well. Both of these support the development of student creativity as an important objective of instruction. Similarly, creativity development–oriented instructional activities represent an entry point to addressing these domains as part of a well-balanced, holistic approach to instruction.

So, how do we address and develop student creativity? There are a variety of approaches educators can take. Importantly, we need to establish a fertile, nourishing environment in which student creativity can emerge and flower. In part, this may include ensuring that the physical elements of the classroom or other learning space encourages students to focus on their creative efforts. Students should be provided places or ways to store projects in progress and share them when appropriate. Of course, when projects are worked on digitally, when finished products or performances are produced and saved, and when these things are shared digitally, such concerns are diminished.

Additionally, we can see to it that resources students may require for their creative efforts, or that may spark creative ideas directly, are available and that students have the necessary support in using them. In supporting the development of student creativity we also need to establish a classroom climate (attitudes, understandings, protocols, rituals, and the like) that supports the creative act, as well.

However, while students may respond to the environment and to the resources available to them as creators, schools principally engender learning by engaging students in activities. Activities and projects are the prime means by which teachers provoke student creativity. Understanding how to structure and implement such activities is key.

While activities for the various types of learning may include a variety of types of things for students to do, a clear view of those activities that we can direct at developing student creativity can be described as challenges.

In her article titled "5 Hallmarks of a Creative Project," Melinda Kolk lists the following five characteristics. A project is creative when it:

1. Asks, or attempts to answer, the right kind of questions

2. Requires collaboration or cooperation

3. Doesn't need the student's name on it

4. Includes original art or design, and

5. Transfers energy and demonstrates passion (Kolk, 2012)

In other words, student projects that involve creativity prompt students to respond to open-ended questions that require something other than a single, correct answer. Involving team work leads to more creativity for more students. The work itself reveals the student's taste and personality, and it appears to be distinct and unique to that student. In addition to new inventions and products, creativity brings joy to our world, makes us smile. According to Kolk, "We work hard on creative projects because they are meaningful and important to us."

How Students Approach Creativity Challenges

Beyond activities, or even full-blown projects, it is useful to view the work in which students are engaged toward the end of developing creativity as challenges. While the nature and composition of student challenges is somewhat fluid, the following dimensions and elements constitute a solid guideline to planning and implementing creativity challenges.

Begin with an open-ended problem or inquiry. In essence, this is a prompt for an activity that asks students to create something that is new and original (to the student). This may be a design and program for a robot to remove a dangerous item from a building, a recipe for a sandwich to celebrate an event, an infomercial to protect an endangered species, a video to teach about the history of an invention, or any number of solutions to quests and problems. Often these prompts are especially impactful because they are contextualized in real world situations.

Often the student will need to research or otherwise gather information. The student will need to find out about the situation that establishes context for the challenge. In the case of a robot designed to enter a building to assist fire fighters, that might include the height and angles of a standard flight of stairs that the robot will have to climb – in developing a recipe, background information might include nutritional values for foods – in creating a public service announcement to save species, the student would likely need to find statistics about endangered animals, understand the threats they face, and its define their survival needs. Students will also want to inform themselves about the history of the problem they are tackling and what other solutions have been tried thus far and how they have fared. Certainly web-based research using search engines like Google will help in accomplishing this, but student may also want to collect, record, and collate and analyze information from their own observations and field measurements. They may find it useful to conduct surveys, to do interviews, and to collect oral histories.

Often the student will be supported by a creative process that guides him through the challenge. If the challenge he is tackling involves creating an infomercial, for instance, he may rely on the writing process and create a storyboard and script as part of his solution. If he is designing a robot, he may follow the engineering process of conceiving a solution, building a prototype, testing it and then refining his design based on the results of a series of tests until he is satisfied that his design works properly. If the student is creating a recipe, he may draw from several processes including the writing process in creating and illustrating the text, a general creative process involving researching other recipes and working through a series of trial batches, gathering feedback from his peers (audience) and refining the final recipe based on them. Familiarity with a few variations of creative process will provide students with a good repertoire of approaches and understandings about how they may contribute to their own creative life; an invaluable form of preparation to create and innovate throughout life.

The student creates a product or produces a performance as the result of working on the challenge, and then presents this at completion of the lesson as the solution or response to the challenge. The learning is enriched greatly by the presence of a real audience for his product or performance, and feedback from that audience deepens the learning.

In a variety of ways, creativity challenges are similar to project-based learning. A good distinction to draw here would be to note that the goal of a creativity challenge is the development of student creativity, whereas the goal of project-based learning is learning. Of course, in the case of either goal there is strong crossover between the two. Often in learning projects students are required to create a product as the focus for their research and learning. And similarly, in nourishing and eliciting student creativity through the type of challenges described here students also produce products. Along with the creativity that is released, students walk away from the experience with a great deal of content knowledge and expanded or freshly acquired skills.

10 Approaches for Learning Activities to Develop Student Creativity

Here's a list of general approaches and tasks that will help students to stretch their thinking and develop their creativity.

1. **Invent something new**—something that doesn't exist yet but that meets a need or purpose, even if it is simply to amuse or amaze.

2. **Repurpose**—take something that exists and make it do something else, make it *be* something new.

3. **Combine things** in new, unthought of, and impossible and wonderful ways.

4. **Solve real-world problems**—how could we get more water? Light up houses without bulbs? Feed the poor?

5. **Consider new solutions and situations**—turn the values of things upside down.

6. **Transform things**—what can we make from all those things we throw away?

7. **Translate things**—painting to sculpture, mechanical to chemical or electronic, inanimate to animate, and so on.

8. **Curate something new** by selecting, collecting, and organizing old things to make something new.

9. **Tell a story differently** (different values, different plot twists, different resolution).

10. **Present a phenomenon or event** from an unconsidered and unique point of view (from perhaps an ant's eye view, a villain's view, and so forth).

Ideas for Activities to Develop Student Creativity

The following are visual art activities that I developed for my own students. These are designed to help students experience their own creativity in a way that enables them to focus on it and discuss it with one another. In addition, when students produce effective visual products they demonstrate their own natural creative abilities to others and themselves.

- Impossible pairings
- Transformations from an image seed
- Pareidolia
- Curated list and variations and expansions
- Digital story math word problem
- Randomized digital story media piece

- Found object sales pitch
- History reenacted
- Student-created textbook
- Informational graphics
- Comic strip
- Rube Goldberg machine
- Sampled music piece
- Doodle from "image seed"

Impossible Pairings: Settings, Marriages, and More

Students will select and present a pairing of images of things (or situations) that seem impossible or poetically unlikely. Either have students find their own "A image" or assign them one from a body of images you've collected for this assignment. Students then engage in imaginative searches, be it via print resources or the internet (e.g., Google Images) to find another image to pair with it. Give the student the prompt, such as "find and display with your starting image another that you feel is either its complete opposite or something that could never be paired with it in real life. Choose something that you feel is both unlikely and that is pleasing because of the way the two things in the images blend. Results might be a palm tree growing on an iceberg, a bird sitting inside a tiger's mouth, a butterfly holding a brick in midflight, or a flower growing from the mouth of cannon."

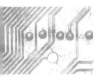

Some well-known art examples of this approach are the paintings of Rene Magritte and the readymades of Marcel Duchamp and Man Ray (like the metronome with a photo of an eye on its arm, *Object to Be Destroyed,* 1923).

Use a digital collage approach for the technique in this project, which is something that all students can accomplish regardless of talent in drawing. After inserting the images into a "canvas" (many word processing programs will work fine for this), students can adjust the images in size, move them about the page, or remove the background around the principal object so that the collage/photo montage aspect of the project can be more easily managed. Alternatively, the final product can be produced as hard copy and either scanned or photographed to produce a digital final product that, in turn, can be posted, shared, and saved permanently.

Transformations from an Image Seed

Have the students "find" an image online as the starting point of this project. Any image, (drawing, photo, and the like) that the student finds highly interesting will do. Following a hunch or area of interest using a search engine will turn up many images the student may start with. After selecting the initial "seed" image, the student's task is to transform it into something else by adding lines, shapes, colors, photos (or segments of photos), and the like. A fun version of this for younger students involves adding limbs and facial features to inanimate objects to create a fanciful creature or a monster. Other students might transform vegetables into machines, tools into portraits, or human figures into landscapes.

Again, a digital collage technique will work fine for this. And, if the original image is inserted into a word processing or PowerPoint (for instance) document, the lines and shapes of the drawing function of those programs will allow students to add a wide variety of design elements that can be applied on top of the original image. Alternatively, after the initial image has been located (perhaps adjusted for size after being inserted into a word processing document) and printed out, conventional art materials can be applied to it. The final product can be scanned or photographed. An interesting example of famous art in this vein are the "Vegetable Man" paintings of Giuseppe Arcimboldo like the one shown in Figure 11.1.

FOUND OBJECTS

A slight variation on the transformation project involves simply locating "found objects" that remind one of something other than their initial, functional identify, and then orienting, displaying, and labeling them with the new, imagined identity. A good example of this would be Picasso's bull created from a bicycle seat and handlebar.

Pareidolia

Pareidolia is a psychological phenomenon involving a visual stimulus from which the mind perceives or suggests a familiar pattern or object that in actuality is not there. The man in the moon is a good example. Da Vinci spoke of seeing faces in clouds or in the texture of rough walls. Artists like Max Ernst would induce this by squeezing paint between a canvas and a piece of paper, leaving rich, irregular patterns of swirls and lines that suggested a great variety of things. Similarly, it is believed that in staring at the rough and irregular walls of caves, Neolithic cave artists saw the suggested images of animals that they would trace with charcoal. This produced famous works of art like those found in the caves of Lascaux.

Pareidolia can be an effective technique with which to demonstrate for students the power of their own mind to produce something from nothing. Provide students with some images of random textures or have them produce their own by squeezing some poster paint between two sheets of paper. Once students have created the image, direct them to look intensely at it until they see something familiar

Figure 11.1 *Reversible Head with Basket of Fruit,* oil on panel by Giuseppe Arcimboldo (c. 1590)

that they can outline and modify. Googling "oil on water" for instance will turn up a great many photos of this nature, as will searching for "patterns in marble or stone," "aerial photo of coral reef," "sand under microscope," and more.

This project may be done entirely digitally or it can be done with conventional pens, pencils, markers, and crayons on a printout of the type of imagery just described. These modified works can then be scanned or photographed to produce a digital file, which in turn may be inserted into a wide variety of media tools to create yet other works that can then be shared or published.

As with all of the projects noted here, having students explain their project, especially in a piece of writing that will accompany the work when it is displayed or published, will enhance the value of the activity in numerous ways.

Curated List

Have students identify a theme on which to create a list. This student choice can easily be aligned to a broad theme taken from required curriculum and standards. The selection of the focus theme, itself, can be an assignment that elicits creative response. Focusing prompts like "choose a theme to investigate that may be surprising or for which you think may result in unusual discoveries while still relating to the broader class theme" will help ensure that the students engage their creativity abilities.

Students next research their theme using common search engines, and then compile a list of items and links to them. Explain to students that they are to create a list and that the number of items they include must conform to a number or range you stipulate. A modest number of items will likely produce the best results as it will permit the students to focus on the creative aspect of the activity and not solely gathering a vast number of things to populate a list. Explain to the students that although their theme is capable of producing a very long and comprehensive list, an abbreviated list better reflects their choices and tastes, and that a short list will, in addition to providing content about their chosen theme, also impart a flavor and sensibility through the focus and taste they exercise in it.

Explain to students further that they are to carefully plan which items to put first, next, last, and so on, and that they are not to use standard format devices like alphabetical order to influence the product they create. The finished list is to be considered as a creative product produced by the student. Curated list projects can be created in any number of ways. Possibilities include:

- **Annotate the list:** Instruct the students to give a short explanatory passage with each of the items they include in their list.

- **Historical/biographical version of the list:** Instruct the students to research and add a quote from a person of fame or note to accompany each of the items on their list.

- **Literary version of the list:** Instruct the students to include a phrase or passage from a book with each of the items on their list. One interesting variation on this might be to have the students interview adults in their lives or neighborhoods, sharing their list of items and requesting that the adult being interviewed give them an idea for such a phrase from a favored author or book.

- **Illustrated version of the list:** Instruct the students to go out on the web using a search engine like Google Images and select an image to insert in their list next to each item that they feel enhances or explains the item. You may want to extend this a bit by having the students explain briefly why they chose their selected images. Students can either keep the explanations separate or incorporate them as part of the document that holds their list.

- **Design the list:** Extend the project by having the students consider the list as a work of art. Have them carefully consider text color, size, placement, and style of each item. The list need not conform to traditional formats of list. For example, students might place each item in their list in a shape (MS Word, for instance, provides many shapes that are easy to insert into a document), and then fill the shape with color or pattern. Students can then move items around the document until each is in a "perfect" location.

Digital Story Math Word Problem

For greater insight into word problems in math, turn the exercise on its head, making the students the creators of the problems. Students can then be challenged to present and explain their word problems to their classmates and peers.

Set a series of criteria for the word problems that your students will create (e.g., no fewer than three mathematical operations to arrive at the answer).

Have the students list the skills and understandings that their audience will be required to know in order to solve the word problem they create.

Have students think of a real-world scenario in which a mathematical solution to a problem presented by the scenarios is required. For instance,

15 kids will attend a party. Each will drink at least 2 cans of cola-flavored soda, but not more than 3. Those who have more than 2, though, will each drink less than half of their third can. Only one third will have more than 2 cans. How many cans of soda must the host purchase for the party?

Randomized Digital Story Media Piece

Digital storytelling is a popular activity and one that clearly corresponds to student creativity. The approach here, though, is primarily focused on tapping, releasing, and highlighting the phenomenon of student creativity, particularly within the context of storytelling. Once students become comfortable and adept with this approach there are many ways that it can be adapted for learning across the curriculum. This approach guides students in exploring and applying several dimensions of creativity that are practical: the generation of multiple possible options for a project element, the adaptation of random elements so that they fit and support the overall project, and similarly, the adaption of the overall project to accommodate a given element that must be incorporated. All of these are common aspects of team creative projects in the current workplace.

Focusing on the elements of storytelling, have students generate a simple story that they feel is of interest.

Set up a table, such as Table 11.1 shown below, that students can use to list options that correspond to the elements of storytelling that you choose to include.

Table 11.1: Storytelling elements for randomized story media piece

CHARACTER Give name and description	SETTING	GOAL	OBSTACLES/ VILLAINS	EVENTS IN THE STORY
JIM a 12-year-old boy				
CLIPPER a stray dog				
JENNY a teenage girl				
BOT a humanoid robot				

Have students choose (or receive by random selection) one element from each column with which to construct a story. This may be done individually or working in pairs. Students should flesh out the stories through discussions in which they describe the action and flow of events in an ordinary conversation voice. They may take notes as they progress, or they may use a digital audio recorder (something commonly included with laptops) to record the discussion. Afterward students can either transcribe the segments they wish to keep and make part of their "finished" story presentation as text, or they can edit the audio recordings and select segments to include in a media-based version. Using a digital canvas provided by a multimedia resource, students can combine images, text, sound, video, and links to online items.

Found Object Sales Pitch

Fill a shoe box with a series of found objects, as well as scissors, a length of twine, tape, staples, and the like that students can use to make a fanciful product. Alternatively, create a digital folder that contains a series of images of objects that students can insert into a digital canvas (e.g., word processing document, multimedia program) with which to produce a fanciful product.

Tell the students that they have a class period (or other relatively short set amount of time) to create something from what they find in their "package" that they will sell to their classmates at the end of the work period. Let students know that their product will be used to illustrate the "thing" they will create to sell, and that they will describe to the group what it is, what it does, and how it works. They should use their imagination—let the found objects suggest to them what they want to be made into. Students should use the power of language and mental imagery, triggered by the object they will create, to fill in the gaps for their audience. Students should focus on what they feel is needed and wanted in the world and create something that satisfies those things.

Next, students can write a script for a TV commercial in which their product is offered to potential buyers. Thus, they are not only creating a product but creating a persuasive argument for its value and need, and then presenting that through the creative use of language to produce the effect of want in potential buyers.

Finally, the commercial can be produced by either having the students present their work in the form of a digital book or slideshow. Students present text with their image(s), or they can produce a video that plays the images and a voice recording of their text.

History Reenacted

Have a class or group of students do background research on a general period or event covered in the required social studies curriculum (e.g., a war, economic development like the Industrial Revolution, or a period of human endeavor like the age of discovery). Direct students to select a single incident within the assigned subject, focusing on character or place that is emblematic of the general theme covered by the class.

Have the students relate essential information about their subject through a dramatic presentation. They should create a character(s) whose life is typical of a person who would have lived during the timeframe of the assigned subject. Students should write a script of dialog in which they share the conditions of the life and events of the character(s). Thinking and speaking as the character they present, students should share their hopes, worries, thoughts, and concerns.

Students may mine the web for images that they feel will help tell their story accurately and convey the feelings of the life of the time they depict.

Explain that they are telling the story of a person from the piece of history they are exploring and encourage students to provide "their audience" with some details from actual life (e.g., food, clothing, and social life). Ask students to imagine how these details may have been influenced by or may have influenced the history they are relating, and how the character(s) may have felt about them.

One dimension of this dramatic retelling of history you may want to include would be to have the student take a still photo of himself or herself as the character created, including, to the extent possible, costume, props, hairstyle, and the like. This may be done at home and brought in to be added to the portfolio of images collected, or this may be done a class event in which students support one another in preparing for and taking their photos.

Student-Created Textbook

Maria, an instructional coach who ran a teacher support center at an inner-city high school in lower Manhattan describes an example of how creativity-based instruction provided the solution for a teacher who was facing a difficult student engagement and discipline problem at that school.

The teacher, a bright and motivated young man, was having difficulty engaging a spirited and highly undisciplined 10th grade class in his history course. After considering both the likely causes for these problems and the strategies for success, this teacher decided to alter his instructional approach to accomplish his standards-based goals through creativity-centered project-based learning. He opted to charge his students with creating their own textbook instead of attempting to force them into compliance with traditional learning as consumers of their commercially published book.

The challenge presented to the students grabbed their attention and deeply engaged them, lending a sense of ownership of the activity and its outcome. It also lent excitement and expectation to the mystery to their learning. They did not know if they could accomplish the task, nor did they know how the textbook might turn out. The students, while given "voice and choice" (an oft-cited guideline for project-based learning) in creating their product, were given specific content to research and explanations to produce. They were also given free rein in how to achieve these goals. Within a set of clearly defined outcomes to ensure quality and coherence, students were left to determine how to organize and format a book that, in turn, reflected their visual and language tastes. The unit was a far greater success than it would have been had this teacher gotten an acceptable level of compliance from the students with a lesson that conformed to the traditional approaches to learning. The students had been disengaged from their learning because they didn't originally see the point of the material, and at their best simply went through the motions of learning simply to satisfy something required of them.

To implement this activity you may not want to let the students see the "standard text" first. A short discussion on what a textbook is and what it is intended to provide is important, though. Essential too is that students are given a comprehensive list and understanding of what content they need to locate and produce (how to give attribution to sources is another important dimension here). Once students know what they must produce they are free (with proper support determined and provided through the guidance of the teacher, of course) to research, analyze discoveries, record, paraphrase, explain, and expand.

Having the class produce a single textbook to which all class members contribute will likely be more practical than having each student create his or her own. Further, a joint effort will ensure consistency of the final project, at least to an appropriate and supportive level. It will also establish a firm platform of inquiry and reflection in which students as members of the entire class, of collaborative groups, and as individuals, can support one another and hold one another intellectually accountable to further the group effort.

Through group meetings a class working on this project can agree on ideals and standards for the formatting and design of their individual pages or sections, which in turn, will function as parts of the class whole project. The freedom to organize and design the content, layout, and function of the textbook makes this project a fertile platform for students to exercise and develop their creativity in the context of a specific application.

For an exciting and highly meaningful variety on this project, have two or more classes work on the same goal individually, reviewing and responding to the work of the other at the end of the project. If the project is given to new classes in subsequent semesters, then the groups involved can benefit from seeing and reviewing the work of preceding groups before being launched in their own effort. It is common practice for writers and generators of content to inform themselves about what has been done on a common theme before they begin their work. Such study will allow students to reflect on that previous work and embrace it as part of their own ongoing effort.

Informational Graphics

Classic, traditional facets of curriculum and learning for numerous subjects that students are required to take include researching, collecting information, gathering data, and analyzing and understanding it in terms of numbers and statistics. Representing these visually is both an effective approach to learning and of communicating and sharing what's been learned. Such representations are also a convenient and powerful entry point to student creativity within the context of learning those subjects.

The elements of choice and expression come into play strongly when students create these representations. The options of pie charts, bar graphs, line graphs, and hybrids, and their details, are plentiful and potentially fascinating. These are indeed forms of visual communication that embraces visual art.

Which form of chart will most functionally represent the quantitative ideas the student is working with? And how may that chart appeal to the eye, how may it most powerfully and clearly illustrate the information it conveys, and what can it communicate emotionally and affectively about its significance to its subject?

Tables offer a great many options, too. Which fields of information are to be included? How should they be organized? Should the table be created on the classical, rectangular grid scheme, or should the student creator break from tradition and try a different way of presenting the information?

Comic Strip

Stories are one of the most basic and elemental manifestations of human creativity. They can be complex in structure, representing the convergence of numerous elements, including character, setting, and plot or the sequence of events that comprise what happens in the story. They can be told through a combination of narration and dialog.

Comic strips represent a sort of storytelling shorthand, for which the creator can tell the story quickly and with economy, but effectively. Drawing and lettering a comic strip is a form of story writing that traditionally has been labor intensive and that required hard-to-acquire skills like drawing, calligraphy, and writing. However, today's digital resources have transformed comics into something that all can do.

Experimenting with these resources alone can spark creativity and inspire users to do something with them to see what their potential is as an artist and storyteller. Allow students to conduct a few experiments, perhaps with prompts, such as: "create a comic strip–based story in which there is a protagonist (principal character) who has a clear goal, a barrier to that goal, and/or a villain who tries to prevent him from achieving it, and a resolution to the story in which the reader finds out if and how the goal was achieved."

Comic strip creation is a powerful activity that can guide students to focus on the nature and craft of storytelling. Some worthwhile approaches and activities directed toward those goals may include:

- Have students reflect on and analyze a well-known or favorite story (such as Goldilocks and the Three Bears), and then retell it using the comic strip format.

- Have students transpose the essential elements of such a story and tell it in an adapted form (Astronaut and the Three Robots, for example).

- Have students pick up on a traditional story and continue the story at a point that takes place after the traditional one has ended.

- Have students attempt to write an original story that is not the retelling of a story that's been told before. Have them present their finished product to peers for feedback in an effort to discover whether or not they avoided retelling all or parts of established stories.

To create comics, have students use an established comic strip resource found on the web. These include Bitstrips and Pixton. Or have them create their own using a word processing resource like MS Word and using the insert image, drawing, and callouts functions. A variety of technology resources increases the palette of elements from which the student comic strip writer/artist may choose.

The comic strip approach to storytelling may be adapted to align with subject area learning. For instance, events from the age of discovery in a social studies class may be retold using comic strips. Well-known scientific discoveries may likewise be told this way. Further, scientific principles may be explained through a narrative in which an anthropomorphized chemical element, property of physics, and so forth may do the explaining in comic strip form.

Chapter 12

Creativity across
the Curriculum

Where will creativity be taught and learned? A very important approach will be to integrate it into the existing instructional program, to make creativity part and parcel of the existing curriculum. This chapter will discuss and give examples of how this can be done in the subject areas of math and science, in ELA and other classes where writing is learned, in visual arts classes, and others.

Math and Science

There are a number of important and exciting approaches to bringing student creativity into teaching and learning in the area of math—these hold true, as well, for science, social studies, and other subjects that aren't often associated with this area of development of the mind. One approach involves using creative writing (and related aspects of literacy learning) and visual art, particularly visual art performing its functions as a communicative, illustrative, and exploratory language, something that can be applied to a great many dimensions of thinking and learning. In addition to this, there are elements of creativity that are uniquely associated with all disciplines, including math, and these can be explored and tapped to develop student creativity and in turn, to better learn math itself through focusing on its creative dimensions.

There are certain dimensions of math learning that have a great deal to do with facets of creativity: problem solving, for instance. Alas, these are often handled by teaching students set routines with which to solve archetypal problems. And the technique for doing this in which they are inculcated is to retrieve from memory the correct routine to plug into the appropriate problem, and then to work through the mechanics of the math involved to come up with a solution. This, no doubt, is far more expedient than supporting and encouraging students to come up with their own approaches or to fully direct their mathematical intelligence at generating a fresh, original way of solving a problem, seeing it through to its conclusion, and then reflecting, evaluating, and retargeting if necessary as part of an ongoing process of thinking and creating mathematically.

Still, there are dimensions of creative problem solving that can be applied to math learning. For instance, the problem solving process can be applied to word problems, a standard and classic element of math instruction.

What happens for many students is that in approaching a word problem they try to recall or to come up with a solution, and if they are stuck in generating one, they are pretty much stuck. By using the problem solving process, they will go through a variety of possibilities, select the most likely one, and then test it out. If it is unsuccessful, they retarget and try something more likely to succeed because it is based on the previous attempt.

Math, itself, is based on the original mathematic concepts and innovations by individuals. In a sense, even our mass education of mathematics can draw on this phenomenon and recapitulate it to a degree for all students. That the original ideas of students may not be original in the absolute sense, that others have come to these ideas, as well, perhaps countless times, for our purpose doesn't matter. The point is that the mathematics abilities and attitudes of students are positively impacted.

The Student as (Math) Teacher Approach

Reversing things, particularly roles in the dance of education, is often a fruitful exercise in creativity. Rather than have the students play the role of individuals who passively receive explanation, students who take on the role of the explainer provide a far greater variety of explanatory material and narrative for the entire class or learning community to "get it" from. Moreover, the act of explaining to others requires a good deal of comprehension and metacognitive reflection of what's to be learned. The act of learning requires creativity to make all of this happen.

This can be seen by turning the word problem issue on its head with students not simply solving and then, perhaps for a more complete experience, explain their solution and how they got to it, but having students create their own word problems. On a simple level, students may "translate" a word problem assigned to them by rewording it and by establishing alternate word imagery. In other words the train travelling at 30 miles per hour can be translated by the student into a herd of deer traveling at a given speed. The successful offering here is something that helps the student visualize the factors and numbers of the problem.

In the Education Week Teacher article "Boosting Creative Thinking in Math Class," teacher Lana Gundy shares a very positive, out of the box teaching experience. In addition to including the full lesson, she says:

> My students usually solve math problems to practice a specific skill. Then we discuss the different ways they approached the problem, helping them understand the skill more deeply. This lesson, however, called for the students to write their own math problems. I knew that, if it was successful, this lesson would get right to the heart of Common Core Mathematical Practice Standard #3, helping my students learn to "construct viable arguments and critique the reasoning of others." (Gundy, 2013)

Odyssey of the Mind (odysseyofthemind.com) is an international educational program that provides creative problem-solving opportunities for students from kindergarten through college. Team members apply their creativity to solve problems that range from building mechanical devices to presenting their own interpretation of literary classics. In addition to student competitions of creative projects the group offers curriculum and activity unit plans, one of which is Made Up Math. This plan guides teachers suggesting that they:

> Introduce creative thinking relative to math to the class. This can include giving meaning to math terms and assigning fun scenarios to equations. For example, a *fraction* can be the number of bites required to eat a candy bar; or the problem, When does 15 - 10 = 1? can be answered in a number of ways (e.g., when a concert ticket costs $15 and you only have $10, it will take one household chore to earn the remaining $5). Ask the class to brainstorm other examples of using creativity to teach math. (Creative Competitions, Inc., 2006)

The ReadWriteThink (www.readwritethink.org) online resource offers recommendations on how to connect two of the most valued and tested content areas, elementary math and literacy, at the same time. This resource provides a number of examples for discussing how creativity can be a learning focus in the context of math. Generally, writing is used as a medium with which to accomplish this. Among the approaches listed are:

- Talking, Writing, and Reasoning: Making Thinking Visible with Math
- Exploring Sets through Math-Related Book Pairs
- Draw a Math Story: From the Concrete to the Symbolic
- Solving the Math Curse: Reading and Writing Math Word Problems

The above activities are all available in the Classroom Resources section of the ReadWriteThink website http://www.readwritethink.org/classroom-resources/

In the article "Where's the L in STEM?" author Jennifer Altieri convincingly points out: "In order for our students to be prepared for STEM careers, they must be able to navigate informational text. This involves understanding text features they rarely encounter in fictional stories. Also, our students must build their vocabulary and strengthen their writing skills. 'STEML' may not flow off the tongue as easily as STEM, but I believe without the L for literacy skills, there is no STEM." (Altieri, 2013)

A snapshot overview of creative literacy connections to math can be had through videos posted that relate to this approach. Some good examples include:

Grapes of Math: youtube.com/watch?v=ZDf1Z_E4jH4

The Boy Who Loved Math, Written by Deborah Heiligman, Narrated by Ms. Meredith, Online Read Aloud: youtube.com/watch?v=Fx2vAdS8f0I

The Greedy Triangle: youtube.com/watch?v=kPuI4XyyZUE

Minnie's Diner—A Multiplying Menu: youtube.com/watch?v=AFDmhd7bqL4

More Math-Literature Connections—Full Video:
youtube.com/watch?v=cGfq0pxD63w&list=PL2BBEDA800C50C7EB

Visual Creativity and Math

Illustration, the visual art of illustration, the explaining and communicating of ideas through images created or selected for that purpose, offers a very rich vein to mine in establishing powerful and practical connections between development of student creativity and math. A convenient entry point for us to explore the intersection of math, visual image creation, and technology is the creation of charts, tables, graphs, and infographics. Those items are designed, visual representations of mathematical information and thus their connections to math are clear. There are powerful ways, though, that other types of art works, ones that are generally seen as more purely expressive than informative, can be used to develop creativity through their application to math instruction.

A body of material of note that is emblematic of using this expressive art-based approach is provided online by The Armory Center for the Arts, an art education organization in Pasadena, California. This material was developed with the support of a U.S. Department of Education grant as a professional development model for t2nd and 3rd grade teachers in partnership with the Pasadena Unified School District.

The Armory's website (armoryarts.org) explains that it "builds on the power of art to transform lives and communities through creating, teaching, and presenting the arts." A number of-activity plans that promote strong connections to creativity through visual art can be found on the page titled "Artful Connections with Math."

Among them is the lesson titled Bar Graph Abstract Painting, which asks: How can we use math and art to show the same data in different ways? In this lesson students create an abstract painting based on the amounts of color in a bar graph they've created. The activity is explained to teachers through a well produced video that demonstrates and illustrates it. The video announces that the activity will teach students how to 1) identify and mix primary and secondary colors, 2) generate and then organize data, and 3) create a painting based on the amounts of color in their bar graph. A clear and standards-based learning goal is established in both the area of visual art and math, and students are provided an opportunity to apply and demonstrate both clearly.

There are over a dozen more of these multi session lessons like: Place Value Sculpture and Fraction Mobile. Each of these is a carefully thought out activity rich in math and visual art content and skills blending both in the production of an art object. While finished student art works like the Place Value Sculpture illustrate and model their targeted mathematics art, the process of planning and preparing to execute the art works walks the students through an effective sequence of instructive stages to learn them, representing a high value instructional experience. Importantly, for each of the lessons offered, there is a detailed video to explain and demonstrate to teachers how to teach the lesson to the students.

Infographics

Infographics is an approach to visual communication that often involves numbers and numerical representations. Some resources of particular worth for engaging students in activities include the following:

Math Giraffe: mathgiraffe.com/blog/infographics-for-education

How Real Kids Create Real Infographics: tinyurl.com/hjuvx2w

Creative Educator/Infographics: tinyurl.com/z7sj858

8 Examples of Incorporating Infographics in Middle School Classrooms: tinyurl.com/jo394ke

New York Times Learning Network blog—Interpreting the Data: 10 Ways to Teach Math and More Using Infographics: tinyurl.com/gpdhh6v

Graphs

Graphs are related to infographics. Graphs are visual representations of numbers, values, and numerical ideas. However they also have a presence as visual art and provide a good opportunity for students to develop and exercise creativity as they explore the intersection of the two. Word processing programs like MS Word provide powerful resources for designing and creating original graphs. There are numerous resources to be found on the web that offer alternative looks and functions for graphs, as well. A good example is the Make Your Own Graphs resource from the Math Is Fun website (mathsisfun.com/data/graphs-index.html).

Resources for Applying Creativity to Math Teaching

The article "How to Use Creative Art Projects to Make Your Students Love Math" by Erin Bittman on the We Are Teachers website (weareteachers.com) shares another rich body of activities that establish the connection between math and creative art projects (Bittman, 2014).

The Math Forum website hosts the resource Creative Geometry (mathforum.org/sanders/creativegeometry/), a deep pool of geometry content and activities that stresses the visual, offering creative connections along the way. In the introduction, math educator Cathleen Sanders explains:

> It is my goal in teaching to introduce students to the creativity and beauty in Mathematics, and to show them the connections between Mathematics and nature, art, science, and all other aspects of their lives. I believe that creative projects can teach students the concepts of mathematics, help them to understand the properties of geometric figures, remember the definitions and theorems in the Geometry curriculum and instill in them an interest in, and perhaps even a passion for, the subject. (National Council of Teachers of Mathematics, 2016)

The Math Forum site also hosts Sanders' free Math Art Connections (mathforum.org/sanders/mathart/), described as "an online class designed to introduce students to many interesting connections between mathematics, art, architecture and design." This is yet another rich repository of ideas, content, and resources align with the theme of creative visual art activities as a complement to mathematics learning.

Some further resources for connecting creativity to math learning include:

ReadWriteThink: Solving the *Math Curse*: Reading and Writing Math Word Problems—a lesson plan for activities based on the book *Math Curse*: tinyurl.com/2d-kjf56. For a quick overview of the *Math Curse* book, see the video: youtube.com/watch?v=0VIk0WFSf2M

P21 Partnership for 21st Century Learning: Write! Camera! Common Core Math!: p21.org/news-events/p21blog/1659

Teaching Channel: Critiquing Reasoning = Rich Math Task: teachingchannel.org/blog/2015/05/22/rich-math-task/

University of Cambridge: Cultivating Creativity: https://nrich.maths.org/5784

Science Items

The approaches discussed in the math section are also highly applicable in the area of science. The connection between visual art is strong, as to how students explain, both to themselves and the learning community of their classroom and beyond, what they have learned. Infographics is one approach with a strong connection across the curriculum. Illustration of concepts and their application in the world is another. Projects to consider might include posters on discoveries, trading cards on famous figures in science, and mock advertisements for inventions or developments. These are the types of activities that not only form a strong connection with visual art-based creativity but establish a powerful real world context.

Directing students to read books relevant to a specific, required curriculum theme and then report on it via a creative project is an approach that will result in powerful content learning. Such an activity will help students develop creativity. Book trailer videos, book discussion group podcasts, and book-based mock movie posters are all exciting and engaging projects of this type.

As is true with mathematics and other subjects, the structure and substance of science education often involves learning bodies of fact and formulas. True, unavoidably, there is a body of science content to be covered and understood which traditionally students have been expected to recall and apply on tests to arbitrary questions and prompts. Still, most of this tested body of fact and skill represents

what, at one time, was the original, creative thinking of those who came before. This tested material covers the history of scientists, and the work and discoveries of these risk-taking individuals. Beyond absorbing what these creative thinkers have achieved, there is also a need for students to walk in their footsteps and to recapitulate the experience and processes by which noteworthy past achievements were accomplished. Further, while those famous achievements represent important questions or problems for which an answer or solution has been established and is now to be "learned," one of the important dimensions of science is that there are multiple possible answers and solutions to be found, some long after the first round of accepted ideas and solutions are recognized.

Putting students into the role of scientist, as opposed to having them fulfill the role of students who study the achievements of a scientist, is a dimension of science education that is established and appreciated, although rarely given the focus and share of attention that it deserves. This dimension of science education engages students as creators and, in the process, develops their creativity or expands it. In the *Science* jounal article "Teaching Creative Science Thinking" Robert DeHaan, professor emeritus at Emory University, says that "if more students learn to think like creative scientists, it will be worth the effort." He goes on to say:

> It's unfortunate that we often teach science as if science only deals with neat problems with a single answer, and a single path to get to that answer. But when you walk into a lab, you don't know what problems you're going to face, or how you're going to arrive at solutions. (DeHaan, 2011)

The article relates that one of DeHaan's favorite creativity-developing exercises, one directed at getting students to think like scientists, is simply "to ask students to list all of the possible uses for an object such as a plastic bottle" (DeHaan, 2011).

Resources for Creativity in the Context of Science Activities

Edutopia: Model Projects: Maker Faire Inspires Learning and Creativity
edutopia.org/maker-faire-DIY-projects

EdWeek Teacher PD Sourcebook: Creative Writing in Science Class. Making up their own stories helps students learn material in fresh ways.
edweek.org/tsb/articles/2008/09/10/01science.h02.html

Creative Little Scientists: Enabling Creativity through Science and Mathematics in Preschool and First Years of Primary Education (funded through the European Union Seventh Framework Programme)
tinyurl.com/zvflshr

Writing

Sometimes, after taking a few steps back to reflect on them, educational problems come into focus as opportunities. Such an opportunity looms before us currently, provided that we can see it clearly and shift our priorities and understandings just a little to take advantage of it. The confluence of our students' very poor level of competence in the skill set of writing, and our nation's overwhelming need to produce innovators, represents just such an opportunity.

The need to improve learning in the area of writing is well established. The Nation's Report Card (2011) shows that only roughly one quarter of eighth and twelfth graders write at the proficient level, with only 3 percent of our students at the advanced level. The remainder scored at either the basic level or below (roughly a fifth) (National Center for Education Statistics, 2012). It must be acknowledged, too, that this is not the result of little attention over the years having been paid to redressing this problem. For a nation that continually asserts it will be internationally influential, if not downright competitive in areas for which writing, is essential, these findings represent a clarion call for trying something different.

The other side of this picture is the need for our schools to produce a sizeable cohort of innovators. President Obama's Educate to Innovate program is indicative of how much of an article of faith it has become that the key to our future is innovation, and that education must prepare students to become innovators. Despite this seemingly sensible belief, in truth our schools do very little to foster creativity as an educational outcome. As an example, our National Science Standards hardly even mention creativity or innovation, let alone provide a framework by which students may develop and demonstrate abilities as innovators. Reflection on this is long overdue, as this is one of those areas for which our assumptions about what we hope to accomplish does not square with reality.

We have before us a "pick up all the marbles and win" opportunity to revamp and revitalize writing instruction as we address the need to foster creativity. By recontextualizing writing instruction, we can both achieve better results and make innovation and creativity achievable educational outcomes.

Upon reflection it becomes clear that creativity and writing are highly connected. So much so that teaching them as dual goals makes a great deal of sense. There are very clear parallels between the two. The writing process, something that language arts teachers and professional writers alike are familiar with, is essentially the same as the design process, something that functions similarly for engineers, inventors, and architects. These STEM field innovators go through the process phases of brainstorming, idea articulation, prototyping, testing and design modification, and finally presenting the finished product. Writers, both professionals and students, similarly go from idea clouds to outlines or storyboards, and then on to drafts that are edited and revised, and ultimately published. What's surprising is that we haven't exploited this connection in our schools more.

How should we transform writing instruction in order to embrace this understanding? First, a distinction must be made between what has been traditionally referred to as creative writing and the creative nature of the subject of writing across the board. Yes, the writing of poems and novels is creative, but truly, all writing can be seen as creative. Perhaps the commonly held belief that functional writing should be taught as a formula-driven chore is one of the reasons we do so poorly with it. Whether it be a book review, business letter, or narrative procedure, the experience of writing can very much be seen as a creative act. Transforming traditional student writing assignments like research reports and reflective essays, items with a considerable presence in our current body of instructional practice, into creative efforts is not much of a stretch. Rather, doing so simply requires an easy shift in context. The point is to make creativity a goal and organizing principle of instruction.

In the real world, creative acts are driven by, focused on, and measured through the products that result and the impact they have. Accordingly, the needed contextual shift to foster creativity and improve writing involves authentic projects. Students should be writing and publishing real products that are intended for an audience who may respond and provide feedback. Closely tied to project based learning, this approach is not unfamiliar to educators; it simply has never been a high priority. Seen in this light, though, that really ought to change.

This transformation in writing instruction is potentially easy to bring about. No major organizational changes are needed in schools. Simply all that is needed is the adoption and high prioritization of authentic student writing and publishing practices and resources. There is a great deal of largely ignored evidence indicating that student writing based on self-identified themes of personal interest and supported by common classroom technology is the key to student engagement. This is an essential and overwhelming missing success factor in the way writing instruction is commonly implemented in our schools. Writing instruction will always be a required part of the curriculum; why not implement it in a manner that is likely to be highly effective?

Beyond schools, student-safe online publications can acknowledge student-created work. Hosting such publications is an easy way for organizations of every stripe to promote and support this critical aspect of the writing process. Doing so provides an energy boost to making learning more relevant. It is in the honoring and valuing of such student work that, to a large degree, the success of this shift will be realized. And what will we do with this Mount Everest of student-created and -published articles, magazines, and books? What a great problem to have! No doubt, there are many ways such a plethora of new content can be folded back into the continuum of reading/writing instruction and enrich it yet further.

The 2004 report "Writing: A Ticket to Work ... or a Ticket Out" conducted by the College Board for the National Commission on Writing states that "a third of all workers fall short of employers' expectations in written communication skills" and that "remedying deficiencies in writing costs American corporations as much as $3.1 billion annually." (College Entrance Examination Board, 2004)

A timeless bit of wisdom states, "if we don't change the direction in which we are heading, undoubtedly we will arrive there!" Fostering creativity and better writing together through the adoption of authentic writing and publishing (writing for real-world purposes, applications, and audiences) as a primary approach to instruction will address and very likely positively impact this critical problem.

In establishing a place and context for developing student creativity, focusing on Writing as a logical and convenient entry point makes good sense. Engaging students in authentic writing/and publishing projects is an easy and convenient opportunity to ensure our students are headed in the right direction as professionals and workers whose success will be supported by their writing abilities. And along with competency in this area, they will develop the creativity skills and understandings that come along with it.

Resources for Creativity in the Context of Writing Activities

Education Digest: Creating Comics Fosters Reading, Writing, and Creativity
tinyurl.com/go668r6

Exploring Women's Creativity—Journaling Into Creativity
womenfolk.com/creativity/journal.htm

Visual Art

It seems natural to assume that what is done in arts courses (visual art and music, primarily, sometimes including creative writing, drama, and dance, as well) is creative. However, in school organizational plans these learning opportunities are often given the status of after-school, Saturday, or summer vacation programs.

Having taught middle school visual art for nearly two decades, it is from deep experience and long-term observation that I assert that this is not necessarily so; art classes don't necessarily see the fostering of creativity as their conscious, intended goal. Often they are planned to teach students "about" art, a generalized goal, that may, at times spark a little creativity or that may engage students in activities that involve a little creativity. However, they also spend a good deal of their allotted time addressing topics that are not specifically intended to develop student creativity as a focus or goal.

Much is done in these classes that has little or nothing directly to do with creativity: technique and craft, history of the discipline, criticism and theory, and more are all part of instruction in the arts. Further, there are activities given in these classes that avoid thrusting students into the challenge of true creativity. Some of these activities have inherent worth other than developing creativity, and others help with classroom management. Such activities include copying the works of famous artists, replicating "model works," producing works within the tight "templated" confines of a set, and engaging in a calculated "project." All of these approaches may have value to offer, but will do very little to foster actual creativity unless given some other spin.

On the other hand, if consciously and purposely designed and calculated by the teacher to trigger or nourish creativity, activities in visual art, music, and other areas can very effectively develop creativity. To accomplish this students need something of a true, open-ended challenge on which to focus.

This is a good point to dispel one of the prevailing myths about creativity, one that actually works against furthering student creativity. This myth is the notion that prompting creative responses requires total freedom of expression. Such a notion is misinformed and is likely to produce disastrous results if taken as the basis for understanding and planning student learning activities intended to foster creativity. For one thing, distributing art materials, be they digital or traditional, and telling students, "Do whatever you want!" is for the most part a recipe for a failed activity. Students typically will experiment for a while, perhaps re-creating something they've done or learned in the past, and then quit, stating that they simply don't know what to do.

On the contrary, assigning students to create a landscape, one that has at least three features in it (at least one manmade, and at least one natural, but with no more than five elements in total), leaves much room for originality. This framework provides enough of a prescribed prompt to get students exploring and working.

Collage

The collage (or visual mashup) is an approach to making visual art that is especially emblematic of an important creative act: combining things, often things that would likely never be paired if not for the artist. It is a process whereby things give meaning, and take on special meaning through the act of combining them.

Collage is an art form that is greatly facilitated by technology. Using a standard word processing program images can be inserted into a document, adjusted for size and orientation, and moved around the page—being positioned and repositioned until their ideal place is found. They can be copied as many times as needed, produced in a variety of sizes, and layered one on top of the other. Images can be made transparent or semitransparent as creative thinking and taste dictate. Internet search engines, especially those like Google Images, can be used to turn up a vast supply and variety of source material. And using image processing functions, either directly in MS Word or in ancillary resources like Google's Picasa, images can be altered, transformed, adjusted, and tweaked in qualities such as color saturation, grain, brightness and darkness, and on and on. All of these manipulations are very easily accomplished by students who may not have any special training, but who do have the desire to create and think creatively.

Above all, collage frees students from the need to possess difficult-to-acquire technical skills in order to produce powerful, meaningful works. Students are free to think and associate and react as their work and its meaning unfold before him or her. This is the creative experience in its essence.

Collage-oriented work can be applied to a wide variety of projects (e.g., posters, trading cards, postcards, books, free standing sculpture, etc.) and can facilitate other opportunities to create across the curriculum.

PART 4

Tools & Resources to Develop Student
CREATIVITY

Technology will not live up to its potential until we start to think of it less like televisions and more like paintbrushes. That is, we need to start seeing computer screens not simply as information machines, but also as a new medium for creative design and expression. The more we learn about the abilities of technology, the more creative we become.

—Saomya Saxena

The following section is intended to help make sense of the overwhelming variety and number of tools that may contribute to developing student creativity. There are far too many to include all of them in this list, or any list for that matter.

Instead, a snapshot of the very full universe of available tools is presented in broad categories intended to make clear the big picture that they form in the aggregate. Further, it is intended to support teachers in selecting the types of resources to be applied in teaching and learning situations and specific items to acquire and use.

Chapter 13

Tools for Creativity

In a sense, any tool or material can be a creativity resource. Picasso created a sculpture of a bull out of an old bicycle seat and handlebars. Hip hop artists use phonograph turntables as musical instruments. Marcel Duchamp recycled a photograph of an eye and a metronome to create a piece of kinetic art. Andy Warhol repurposed soup can labels as fine art prints. In fact, repurposing things for new uses, along with combining things in ways previously unconsidered, are essential acts of creating. If we investigate and reflect, we can see that such resources are originally intended to be used for purposes other than creativity. It is the creative act that makes them creativity resources. Similarly, many things are somewhat creativity neutral. For instance, a notebook of ruled paper can be used for keeping lists of laundry or items to buy at the supermarket, or it can be the platform on which a novel is written. A package of school crayons can be used simply to fill in fields of color in an already printed outline drawing as a simple amusement for kids, or it can be the medium for a powerful work of art based on a highly inventive, original image.

Conversely, some resources are intended, or at the very least labeled and marketed, as creativity resources. Certainly, digital cameras and recording devices, as well as associated software intended to refine and extend what can be produced with them, can be considered creativity resources. Still, it isn't very challenging to understand that such resources alone will not result in products or performances that are truly or even broadly considered to be creative. It is the intention behind their use and the understanding of creativity during their use that will result in creative things emerging from their use. There's no magic to be had from resources themselves. The resource itself won't make the creativity happen. It is the creator who creates. The resource merely enables and facilitates an artist's creation.

Creativity tools can be digital resources; such resources can do a great deal. They cannot, however, on their own, at least, make students creative. However, they can perform the following valuable functions toward developing student creativity. They can:

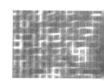

- Guide and kick-start thinking, which is useful for generating ideas, analyzing, organizing, recording, and sharing them.

- Support creativity by providing a sandbox, playground, or laboratory for student trial and experimentation.

- Provide a canvas that allows students to define and communicate their ideas and products.

- Provide a medium or allow students to work with a medium to communicate ideas and deliver products and performances.

One of the wonderful things about these tools is that they tend to be intuitive, easy to use, easy to access, and are often either free or already available in the resource set that comes standard with devices.

Apart from using the tools and resources listed here, a simple online search will turn up a great many options. Further, as researching and acquiring resources for students to use in their creativity efforts becomes part of your ongoing practice it may prove wise to avail yourself of websites that provide comprehensive listings, descriptions, and reviews of digital resources. A few noteworthy examples are:

EdTech Digest's Cool Tools section
edtechdigest.wordpress.com/features-2/cool-tools

Free Technology for Teachers
freetech4teachers.com

Graphite, a resource from Common Sense Media
graphite.org/top-picks/design-thinking-tools-for-students

Cool Tools for Schools, a searchable collection of digital tools, many of value for student creativity efforts

cooltoolsforschools.wikispaces.com/Tools+at+a+glance

Like the resources themselves, there are numerous other sites that list and advise on resources. New ones crop up periodically.

Creativity and Thinking Tools

What sets the proposition of developing students as creative individuals currently apart from the same need and possibility as experienced in the past is the emergence of resources that are available to support them. The emergence of digital resources that have been developed for specific purposes relating to creativity and that are designed to increase the user's understanding of tasks at hand as well as make them easier to perform and, above all, extend his capabilities changes things strongly. In many ways all individuals now can develop and apply their creativity and there are easy to acquire, easy to use digital resources for support. This section shares imagination tools, resources designed to suggest starting places, provoke thoughts and making inspired connections. These are fun and easy items quickly immerse students in the context of creativity. There is also a subsection titled creative thinking tools that presents a wide variety of resources designed to help with the heavy lifting involved in creative projects. These aid in visualization and organization of information and ideas, and in early experimentation with possible approaches to creating responses and solutions to problems and prompts that constitute assignments and challenges set before students.

Imagination Tools

Fodey.com (fodey.com/generators). This site allows you to choose from objects like talking squirrels, flowers, cats, and much more. You can then make an animation that delivers whatever you type into the screen. Although this tool is very simple, younger kids will enjoy the quickness at which they can create something. You can even download the images you create and share them with your friends.

Klowdz (klowdz.com). This resource lets you unleash your creative cloud shape hunting skills and share them with the world. Pick from a large number of "blank" clouds, imagine and draw, then save and share. You'll need an HTML5-compatible browser to draw with Klowdz.

Build Your Wild Self (buildyourwildself.com). An enchanting mixture of elf/fairy-like graphics and interesting scientific information makes this a great little application to explore with children of many ages. Build a "you" then add animal characteristics that transport you into a world of fantastic creatures and beyond.

Switch Zoo (switcheroozoo.com). Make new animals, play games, solve jigsaw puzzles, learn about animals, join a zoo quest, watch movies, and more.

Creative Thinking Tools

Idea Champions (ideachampions.com/jump_start_new.shtml). This resource offers several interactive creative thinking engine resources, including Jump Start, which works as a catalytic spark generator, a quick way to get started on a creative effort.

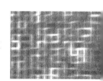

Lino (linoit.com). This site offers a free brainstorming tool that functions like Post-it notes.

Niice (niice.co). A beautifully simple tool to create moodboards.

GroupMap (groupmap.com). Specifically built to make team activities easy, providing a unique platform for anyone to respond on a map, with any parameters you set. You can select a map or create your own, and then invite your team to collaborate, comment, converse, and vote to help decide the best ideas from a session. Each individual can add their ideas to the brainstorm, and the results aggregate into a group view for comments and voting, making for a more open, efficient process.

Popplet (popplet.com). A free online tool that allows you to create mind mapping and brainstorming diagrams. You may create a maximum of 5 Popplets.

MindMeister (mindmeister.com). The leading online mind mapping application, MindMeister allows your team to be more innovative by providing a shared collaboration and brainstorming environment on the web. Plan projects, manage meetings, and sketch out business plans online with partners and colleagues, all in real time.

SpiderScribe (spiderscribe.net). An online mind mapping and brainstorming tool. It lets you organize your ideas by connecting notes, files, calendar events, and the like in free-form maps. You can collaborate and share those maps online.

Bubbl.us (bubbl.us). A simple and free web application that lets you brainstorm online. You can create colorful mind maps online, share and work with friends, embed your mind map in your blog or website, email and print your mind map, and save your mind map as an image.

Text2MindMap (text2mindmap.com). This tool allows the input of text for the organization and creation of mind maps.

Scapple (literatureandlatte.com/scapple.php). An easy-to-use tool for getting ideas down as quickly as possible and making connections between them. It allows you to make notes anywhere on the page and to connect them using straight dotted lines or arrows.

Mind42 (http://mind42.com). This resource provides free, fast, simple mind mapping.

Lucidchart (lucidchart.com). A web-based diagramming software that allows users to collaborate and work together in real time to create flowcharts, organizational charts, and mind maps.

Mind Tools (mindtools.com). While not specifically developed for education, the Mind Tools website, directed at the world of business and career, offers a well-thought-out overview of creativity techniques and how they are implemented with and without the support of digital resources. While the free side of the site offers only a smattering of links to such resources, it does identify and define a wide variety of creativity activity and technique concepts as well as provide information about them. An online search based on this information will likely provide links to tools based on the same or very similar ideas.

Wise Mapping (wisemapping.com). Free online mind mapping editor. This web mind mapping tool leverages the power of Mind Maps, mixing new technologies like HTML 5.0 and SVG.

Composing Tools

Composing tools are the workhorses of activities planned to develop student creativity. Despite the value of the learning environment, in the end, students must generate products and performances that guide them in focusing on creative work and demonstrating their learning and creativity. In other words to be creative, they must create. In encouraging creative work from students, providing them with a choice of appealing and easy to use resources with which to generate attractive and expressive items that effectively capture and transmit their personality, preferences, interests, and Creativity is important. Providing multiple means and multiple media is also an approach that will likely engage more students successfully. To that end a good sampling by type and specific example is provided below.

Visual Communication and Visual Art Tools

Infographics are loved by all since they represent data in a colorful and catchy way. By using free tools for infographics, students can create awesome graphs, which make the interpretation of information easier and quicker. They can employ their creativity and imagination to create an infographic about a topic, concept, or anything they want. They can share these infographics and also embed them into their classroom blog. This encourages and fosters creativity in students. Some free tools for creating infographics include the following.

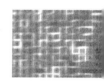

Online Chart Tool (onlinecharttool.com). This tool can help you design and share your own charts online, and for free. The tool supports a number of different chart types like: bar charts, pie charts, line charts, bubble charts, and radar plots.

Piktochart (piktochart.com). Students can use Piktochart to display data in infographics or tell a story using images.

Easel.ly (easel.ly). A template driven resource to create powerful infographics. Can support students in understanding and creating infographics, and can model independent efforts in the process.

Infogram (infogr.am). Create and publish beautiful visualizations of your data. Interactive, responsive, and engaging.

Gliffy (gliffy.com). Create flowcharts, floor plans, and technical renderings with ease. Gliffy helps you organize your thoughts and collaborate with anyone that has access to a web browser.

MoMA Art Lab (moma.org/explore/mobile/artlabapp). A free app for any budding artist or art enthusiast. It includes drawing and collage tools, art inspiration, art activities, a camera for screen capture, and a gallery. MoMA Art Lab lets students take a virtual trip to the Museum of Modern Art without going to New York City.

Visual Arts Units blog (visualartunits.blogspot.com). Posts by the author include many practices and free visual art resources.

Paper by FiftyThree (fiftythree.com). A breakthrough simple way to take notes with touch. Swipe right to create checklists, left to create titles. Put a little fun in getting stuff done. Draw on photos or quickly spotlight details. Create sharp diagrams, charts, and drawings with Paper's world-class tools. Nobody has to know you're not at your desk.

PicMonkey (picmonkey.com). Photo editing and graphic design tool is a good choice for older students, allowing them to create images and experiment with basic graphic design.

QVectors (qvectors.net). QVectors has free, quality vector images that will fit student needs.

MorgueFile (morguefile.com). Looking for high resolution stock photos for your illustration, comp, or design needs? Search morgueFile for free reference images.

Adobe Photoshop Elements (photoshop.com/products/photoshopelements). Go from so-so snapshots to forever favorite photos with Photoshop Elements software.

Art Studio Chalkboard (studiochalkboard.evansville.edu/indax.html). Assists artists with the technical fundamentals of painting and drawing. Created specifically for art students, this online source teaches shading, color, and, perspective.

FreeStockPhotos (freestockphotos.com). Just as the name implies, FreeStockPhotos is an excellent resource to find photos for digital projects. Photos include a variety of landscapes—from weather and flowers to Athens and Egypt.

Snapseed (itunes.apple.com/us/app/snapseed/id439438619?mt=8). This app brings to your mobile device the power and control of professional photo editing software, previously only available on the desktop. Now with the tap of a finger you can retouch, adjust perspective, re-edit, and more.

Music Composing Tools

iTooch Music (edupad.com/itooch/seventh-eighth-grade-music-app/) A comprehensive, interactive application to enhance or supplement middle school music curriculum. In each section of the app, kids can explore lesson text, answer practice quiz questions, and learn about music theory. When in test mode, students receive a grade and earn points toward increasingly colorful martial-arts-inspired belts, adding to the balance of fun and serious content in the app.

UJAM (ujam.com/ujamstudio). Make music. Send greetings. Get creative. Create your own song, send musical greetings or remix songs.

Music Mixer (kids.nationalgeographic.com/games/more-games/music-mixer). Provided by National Geographic Kids. Students can form a virtual band by mixing different sounds and effects.

Incredibox (incredibox.com). Students explore musical elements, create their own musical tracks, and create a video for it using a variety of easy to use design resources.

Sock Puppets (itunes.apple.com/us/app/sock-puppets/id394504903?mt=8). Sock Puppets lets you create your own lip-synched videos and share them on Facebook and YouTube. Add puppets, props, scenery, and backgrounds and start creating. Hit the record button and the puppets automatically lip-synch to your voice.

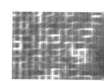

Digital Video and Audio, and Animation Tools

Video, Audio, and Animation are media types and content formats that students are much involved in. They constitute a good portion of the information and entertainment that students consume continually. This familiarity not only establishes a receptivity, but a sophistication and a high level of expectation for resources with which to produce their own content. While there is a great abundance of digital media tools available, included below is a selection that includes examples capable of serving young students in generating products in the areas of Video, Audio, and Animation that are appropriately easy to use without much training and practice. Students use these to generate audio podcasts and online videos that will serve as creative products for a wide variety of themes and instructional purposes that can either be posted directly or embedded in blogs, media mash-ups, websites or other online publishing formats.

Audio-recording tools

SpeakPipe (speakpipe.com/voice-recorder). Allows you to create an audio recording directly from a browser by using a microphone. The recording is produced locally on your computer, and you can record as many times as you need. There is the option to save your recording on the SpeakPipe server and get a link to it, so you can send it via email or use on the web. Works on iPhone, iPad, iPod, and Android devices.

Vocaroo (vocaroo.com). Provides simple online voice recording.

AudioPal (audiopal.com). Create and upload audio files by recording through phone, mic, or by using text-to-speech.

Record MP3 (recordmp3online.com). Record your voice using the recorder. When you have finished an audio player will appear. You can download the file, or upload it to a Dropbox account. If you are using a smartphone or tablet, click the button and either record audio or video and the site will convert it to MP3 for you.

Video Creation Tools

Students may create videos through the use of animation resources, through the practice of capturing virtual screen events, and by transforming existing materials in a variety of formats to video. The following section lists types of resources that students may use to produce videos and several varieties of each type. In our video-driven world, no collection of tools to make available to students to encourage and support their creative work would be complete without a couple to generate videos. Not only are videos directly the format of choice for many student creative products, but they are also a valuable resource to use in documenting the process of creating student products that are done in other formats, as well as capturing student reflections on the experience of producing them.

Animation

GoAnimate for Schools (goanimate4schools.com). An easy-to-use resource that supports students in creating a wide variety of animations.

Do Ink app (doink.com). Easy drawing, animation, and green screen resources.

Explee (explee.com). Create your own animated video.

Zimmer Twins (zimmertwins.com). Students can create and share their own animated stories.

Funimate (funimate.com). Create surprisingly fun looping videos with music. Add text and music to your Funimate, be the star of your own music clip, and easily share it on popular social networks.

Wideo (http://wideo.co/en/) Create, edit, and share animated videos with this unique platform.

Moviesandbox (moviesandbox.net). Allows you to quickly sketch and animate 3D characters and props. Its focus is on ease of use and modularity. The idea is that you can simply draw objects in 3D space and animate them with the built-in timeline.

Video Screen Capture Tools

Jing (techsmith.com/jing). Select any window or region that you would like to record, and Jing will capture everything that happens in that area. From simple mouse movements to a fully narrated tutorial, Jing records everything you see and do. And then the tool lets you share your videos with anyone.

Screenr (screenr.com). A web-based screen recorder that makes it easy to record your screen activity and share it on the web.

Video Resources

Magisto (magisto.com). Turns your everyday videos and photos into exciting, memorable movies you'll want to watch again and again.

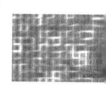

GIF Brewery (gifbrewery.com). Convert your video files into animated GIF images, which you can use on your blog or tweets.

Animoto (animoto.com). Creative, easy-to-use tool for making and sharing videos.

Microsoft Hyperlapse (research.microsoft.com/en-us/um/redmond/projects/hyperlapseapps). Creates smooth and stabilized time lapses from first-person videos. Want to show your friends what you saw on that 12-mile hike you took last weekend or let them experience how it felt to fly down the mountain on your recent ski trip? With Microsoft Hyperlapse, you can time lapse those experiences, distilling them into an easily consumable, enjoyable experience.

Replay app (replayapp.com). Offers easy video editing from your phone. It offers added motion graphics, music, and other enhancements.

PicPlayPost (http://www.mixcord.co/partners/picplaypost.html) Use #PicPlayPost to create video collages and share your captivating stories using photos, videos, GIFs, and music. Available through iTunes app store.

Multi-Media Mashup Tools

Wixie (wixie.com). An online publishing and creativity platform that lets students share what they know through their writing, their voice, and their art.

Buncee (buncee.com). A perfect tool for students to share their learning and express their creativity. Buncee provides students the opportunity to be self-directed content producers. Students can tell their own stories with ease, adding images, video, and recorded voice that personalizes their story. Buncee helps students make connections with content through graphics, cited images, audio, video, and links. Students can include their own drawings, and they can publish and share their work in a variety of ways.

Glogster (glogster.com). Create multimedia digital posters to tell a story.

Curation Tools

Podsnack (podsnack.com). Lets the user create a playlist of recordings. A link is created to the podsnack that can be handed in as an assignment. It also provides an embed code to the podsnack if you want to add it to a website or eportfolio to show evidence of growth.

Diigo (diigo.com). This is a multi-tool for personal knowledge management. Its goal is to dramatically improve workflow and productivity. This tool is easy and intuitive, yet versatile and powerful.

Journaling and Portfolio Tools

Seesaw (http://web.seesaw.me/) empowers students of any age to independently document what they are learning at school. Students capture learning with photos and videos of physical work, or by adding digital creations. Everything is uploaded and kept organized for teachers. Teachers can invite families to Seesaw so parents get an immediate, personalized window into their child's learning. A review can be found at web.seesaw.me and an overview at https://youtu.be/tlw-tUKvnNc

Notability (gingerlabs.com). Combines handwriting, photos, and typing to bring your projects to life. Add as much detail as you like with a variety of colors and fonts.

Google Docs (docs.google.com). Online document creation and storing resource that allows users to share documents for group work. Smart editing and styling tools help users easily format text and paragraphs. Choose from hundreds of fonts, add links, images, and drawings. All for free.

Google Drive (drive.google.com). Offers 15 GB of free Google online storage, so you can keep photos, stories, designs, drawings, recordings, videos, and more.

Blogger (blogger.com). This is a free blogging resource from Google that can be used for student journaling.

OneNote (onenote.com). This is a free digital notebook that is great for journaling. There is an iPad app. The differentiator between OneNote and other similar resources is that OneNote allows for handwriting. Students can insert a picture from an experiment/project and then annotate it with their own handwriting, or students can draw on the page itself. OneNote also includes the Office Lens feature, which turns the iPad into a portable scanner, allowing students to take pictures of handouts, posters, or whiteboard drawings.

Presentation Tools

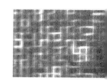

Adobe Voice (tinyurl.com/lmmmlh5). No filming—just talk to tell your story, import or pick from thousands of beautiful images and icons, and watch the amazing cinematic results.

Meerkat (time.com/3742746/meerkat). Livestreaming app on Twitter.

Storytelling Tools

Bitstrips (bitstrips.com). Offers a free 30-day trial that comes preloaded with a variety of layouts, clip art options, and text bubbles. It's also available as an app in Google Play and the Apple app store.

ToonDoo (toondoo.com). Use this tool to quickly make customized comic strips and cartoons.

Booktrack Classroom (booktrackclassroom.com). Add audio tracks to ebooks, like sound effects, music, or even spoken words to make the stories come to life.

Strip Generator (stripgenerator.com/strip/create). Create comic strips with ease.

Toontastic (http://launchpadtoys.com/). Toontastic is used in kindergarten through high school. Several students can collaborate on the same story. Completed cartoons can be shared online or saved for use in other projects.

TeleStory (https://itunes.apple.com/us/app/telestory/id915378506?mt=8) An augmented reality video camera that lets students run wild with their imagination. It lets kids write and record a story in a number of fun themes like a news report, a space adventure, or a spy movie. Using augmented reality, students become a part of the story themselves with a variety of fun video effects, and can even switch between cameras to vary the action.

Storybird (storybird.com). Simple tools help students build books in minutes. The art provided by the tool can inspire students as they write.

My StoryMaker (carnegielibrary.org/kids/storymaker). Easy digital storytelling for even very young students. Limited to the provided palette of characters and plot elements, but still an enchanting digital storytelling tool that has many creativity development capabilities.

StoryLines for Schools (tinyurl.com/jkddznj). StoryLines is an award-winning, collaborative game that helps students learn and master language arts skills aligned to the Common Core. It allows students to play a creative game of "telephone" with others from around the world to improve vocabulary and language proficiency.

ZooBurst (zooburst.com). This is a digital storytelling tool that lets anyone easily create his or her own 3D pop-up books.

We Make Stories (wemakestories.wikispaces.com). Create a storybook online and share it with others. Easy to use for even young students.

Sharing and Publishing Tools

One of the great challenges in educating today's connected students is establishing and communicating to them that learning activities are relevant. Personalized learning is connected to relevance; project-based learning, as well. Fostering sudent creativity, too, is something that requires the students to sense relevance. Conversely, the opportunity for students to be creative is a dimension of school activities that establishes relevance, bringing along with it the benefits of heightened student motivation and engagement. One powerful way to establish relevance in student projects is to have students create products to present to a real audience. This supports various dimensions of learning as it likely involves presenting one's work to peer classmates, eliciting feedback on which to base refinements of the work and offering feedback to support others in refining theirs. Even better though, when the audience includes more than simply classmates and can be drawn from the extended school community and beyond, perhaps far beyond out in the real world outside the school. The audience becomes larger and less familiar, taking on increased significance. Today's media and social publishing resources allow students to present work that appears professional in sophisticated ways to a vast possible audience, one that may be enticed to offer valuable feedback and acknowledgement. The following section highlights a number of resources and opportunities for students to publish their work.

Publishers of Student Work and Student Publishing

Writing Challenge for Kids (tinyurl.com/h2zq23p). Creative prompts and ideas that are designed to spark children's inspiration and creativity.

Basic Language Literacy (noodletools.com/debbie/literacies/basic/yngwrite.html). Online opportunities for young writers.

Figment (figment.com). Teen writers express themselves on this supportive social site.

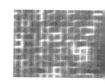

ePubBud (epubbud.com). A website created by two parents of a boy named Wren who died 12 hours after his birth. The website was created so that they could write an ebook about their experience that would be available on iPad. The website functions much like YouTube for children's ebooks.

Book Writer App (tinyurl.com/hpzdutp). Allows students to create their own ebooks.

Flipsnack (flipsnack.com). A free online app that allows you to convert images into digital books with a professional look and the ability to flip through pages.

Student and Class Blogging

Blogs offer students numerous opportunities to develop and focus on their creativity. Blogs streamline the extended process continuum of writing (a thinking process), publishing, and giving and receiving feedback on what's been written. The formats of current blog resources embrace and allow for the embedding of images (photos, drawings, graphics, and the like), audio and video widgets/players, and other digital media varieties. Popular choices include Edublogs, WordPress, and many more. There are also a number of other interesting technologies in this area.

Wordfaire (wordfaire.com). A simple and free live-blogging platform that updates in real time.

Kidblog (kidblog.org) Kidblog gives students' writing a meaningful purpose and an authentic audience. Students are motivated to write for their peers and engage with a global network.

Blogger in the Classroom (www.google.com/educators/activities/pdfs_GTA/CribSheet.Blogger3.pdf) Blogger makes it easy for students to share schoolwork with their peers, parents, and others and to collaborate on projects and get feedback.

SlideShare (slideshare.net). An online community that allows users to upload, download, and share slideshows with each other.

Other Miscellaneous Tools

To finish this section here's a small smattering of other resources, ones that don't fit neatly into any of the categories above. These all offer something to spark the imagination, get students actively creating, and thinking out of the box, in general. These can be used on their own when a little creativity is needed to balance the day, or as opening, warm-up activities before launching into an extended activity in which students will be called on to tap into their creativity.

Adventure Story Starters (scholastic.com/teachers/story-starters/adventure-writing-prompts). This interactive tool randomly generates a story idea when students spin the wheel.

Puzzlemaker (discoveryeducation.com/free-puzzlemaker). Students can create their own word searches, crosswords, mazes, and more.

DIY (diy.org). The Maker community celebrates skill building and creativity. This site provides many opportunities for students to participate in broad-based challenges, to post their efforts on the web, and to give and receive feedback from peers and like-minded others.

Stick Around app (http://learninginhand.com/stickaround/) Students make their own functional sorting and labeling puzzles they can play, design, and share. Students use drawing tools and imported photos to create a diagram or image that they label using fun stickers and text. This is a great alternative to prepared worksheets and reproducibles as it has students create their own, thereby helping them learn targeted content as they experience and learn approaches to creativity.

Chapter 14

Resources

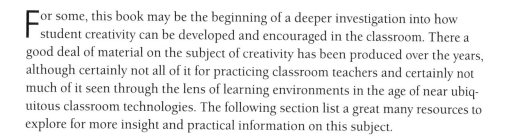

For some, this book may be the beginning of a deeper investigation into how student creativity can be developed and encouraged in the classroom. There a good deal of material on the subject of creativity has been produced over the years, although certainly not all of it for practicing classroom teachers and certainly not much of it seen through the lens of learning environments in the age of near ubiquitous classroom technologies. The following section list a great many resources to explore for more insight and practical information on this subject.

Books, Essays, and Articles on Creativity and Teaching Creativity

May, Rollo. *The Courage to Create*. 1975. New York: W. W Norton & Company. Published in 1975, this book by noted psychologist Dr. Rollo May offers many useful insights and reflections on the phenomenon of creativity. PDF version available at http://goo.gl/kioHJ3.

Center for Childhood Creativity. *Executive Summary: Inspiring a Generation to Create: Critical Components of Creativity in Children*, 2015. Four-page research paper that addresses the questions, "What are the processes or skills that are developing in children that contribute to their creativity?" and "What environments, opportunities and types of adult and peer interactions foster the development of these skills?" http://goo.gl/6qFSOO.

Crossman, Donna C., "Fostering Creativity Within the Classroom" (2013). Creative Studies Graduate Student Master's Projects. Paper 188. A teacher's in-depth investigation into refining her practice to foster student creativity. http://goo.gl/dHreT6.

Beghetto, Ronald A. "Does Assessment Kill Student Creativity?" *The Educational Forum*, Volume 69, Spring 2005. An educator's reflections and experience in understanding and strategizing the assessment process within the context of instruction to develop student creativity. http://files.eric.ed.gov/fulltext/EJ683512.pdf.

DeBord, Karen. "Child Development: Creativity in Young Children." 1997. North Carolina Cooperative Extension Service. An introductory overview of the prospect of addressing fostering student creativity from the child development perspective. www.ces.ncsu.edu/depts/fcs/pdfs/fcs470.pdf.

Loveless, Avril M. "Creativity, technology and learning—a review of recent literature" Futurelab (2007). This organized literature review presents many pedagogical perspectives and ideas still relevant today http://goo.gl/pqU5HI.

Cochran, David. "The New Bloom's Taxonomy," Creative Educator (online). A discussion of the implications of the revised Bloom's taxonomy on planning and implementing instructional projects www.thecreativeeducator.com/v02/articles/The_New_Blooms.

Clifford, Miriam. "30 Ways To Promote Creativity in Your Classroom" (2013) Clifford Innovation Excellence online. An overview discussion of the state and importance of instruction to develop student creativity with numerous approaches and strategies for teachers www.innovationexcellence.com/blog/2013/01/10/30-ways-to-promote-creativity-in-your-classroom.

"Tips for Cultivating Innovative Thinking in Your Classroom" (2014) PBS & WGBH Educational Foundation. https://edtechdigest.wordpress.com/2014/02/05/tips-for-cultivating-innovative-thinking.

What Does Innovation Really Mean? A suite of Informational Materials for teachers from PBS Learning Media www.pbslearningmedia.org/collection/innovation.

Melinda Kolk, "5 Hallmarks of a Creative Classroom Project" (2012) Creative Educator online. A discussion of instructional projects that tap student creativity as they teach required curriculum and content http://goo.gl/pqU5Hl.

Porter, Bernajean. "Digital Storytelling Across the Curriculum: Finding content's deeper meaning" tech4learning.com. Discussion on dimensions of digital storytelling as an instructional approach with numerous references to student creativity www.digitales.us/wp-content/uploads/2015/07/Digital_Storytelling_in_the_Classroom.pdf.

Thai, A. & A. Russell, A (2010) "Tech Supported Tools to Foster Kids Creativity" A blog post and table that analyzes the evolving mass of digital tools and resources suitable for student creativity use www.joanganzcooneycenter.org/2010/08/23/tech-supported-tools-to-foster-kids-creativity.

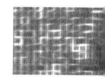

Videos about Creativity

Where Does Creativity Hide? | Amy Tan | TED Talks: youtube.com/watch?v=8D0pwe4vaQo

Your Elusive Creative Genius | Elizabeth Gilbert | TED Talks: youtube.com/watch?v=86x-u-tz0MA

Ken Robinson at Miami school Daily Edventures - Anthony Salcito Interviews Sir Ken Robinson at Miami Global Forum: youtube.com/watch?v=-2d4lHAE9Fo

Sir Ken Robinson - Can Creativity Be Taught?: youtube.com/watch?v=vlBpDggX3iE

Sir Ken Robinson, Creativity, Learning & the Curriculum: youtube.com/watch?v=9X0CESnGQ8U

Sir Ken Robinson on Common Core, Creativity, & Technology in the Classroom: youtube.com/watch?v=SdrzDIUxVP0

Creative thinking - how to get out of the box and generate ideas: Giovanni Corazza at TEDxRoma: youtube.com/watch?v=bEusrD8g-dM

The art of innovation | Guy Kawasaki | TEDxBerkeley: youtube.com/watch?v=Mtjatz9r-Vc

Our approach to innovation is dead wrong | Diana Kander | TEDxKC: youtube.com/watch?v=pii8tTx1UYM

A crash course in creativity: Tina Seelig at TEDxStanford:
youtube.com/watch?v=gyM6rx69iqg

TEDxDoha - Taika Waititi - The Art of Creativity:
youtube.com/watch?v=pL71KhNmnls

Creativity as a Life Skill: Gerard Puccio at TEDxGramercy:
youtube.com/watch?v=ltPAsp71rml

7 steps of creative thinking: Raphael DiLuzio at TEDxDirigo:
youtube.com/watch?v=MRD-4Tz60KE

Creativity Under Pressure: Todd Henry at TEDxXavierUniversity:
youtube.com/watch?v=7hWRva_sPeE

Learning to Risk. Risking to Learn: Victor Saad at TEDxWindyCity:
youtube.com/watch?v=-wA2aR0wDVo

The Art of Teaching Entrepreneurship and Innovation: Tina Seelig:
youtube.com/watch?v=hCTqKSVT7Uk

Everything Is A Remix (Full Film):
youtube.com/watch?v=coGpmA4saEk

How To Be Creative | Off Book | PBS Digital Studios:
youtube.com/watch?v=welQIthC3Ks

Teaching art or teaching to think like an artist? | Cindy Foley | TEDxColumbus:
youtube.com/watch?v=ZcFRfJb2ONk

Tina Seelig: The 6 Characteristics of Truly Creative People:
youtube.com/watch?v=CgCdsERkqrc

Tony Wagner - Creating Innovators:
youtube.com/watch?v=IE6-u6N5oE8

References

Adams, S. (2013). *The 10 skills employers most want in 20-something employees.* Retrieved from www.forbes.com/sites/susanadams/2013/10/11/the-10-skills-employers-most-want-in-20-something-employees/

Adobe Systems, Inc. (2016). *Nine years of Adobe Youth Voices.* Retrieved from www.adobe.com/corporate-responsibility/education/adobe-youth-voices.html

Adobe Systems, Inc. (2013). *Barriers to creativity in education: Educators and parents grade the system.* Retrieved from www.adobe.com/content/dam/Adobe/en/education/pdfs/barriers-to-creativity-in-education-study.pdf

Alber, R. (2012). *Deeper Learning: A Collaborative Classroom Is Key.* Retrieved from www.edutopia.org/blog/deeper-learning-collaboration-key-rebecca-alber

Altieri, J. (2013). *Where's the L in STEM?* | International Literacy Association. Retrieved from http://literacyworldwide.org/blog/literacy-daily/2013/02/05/where-s-the-l-in-stem-

wApple Classrooms of Tomorrow. (2016). *Culture of innovation and creativity.* Retrieved from http://ali.apple.com/acot2/innovation/

References

Avasthi, A. (2008). *Video games can make us creative if spark is right* | Penn State University. Retrieved from http://news.psu.edu/story/187826/2008/05/23/video-games-can-make-us-creative-if-spark-right

Azzam, A. M. (2009). Why creativity now? A conversation with Sir Ken Robinson. *Educational Leadership, 67*(1), 22-26.

Barras, C. (2014). *Can you learn to be creative?* | BBC Future. Retrieved from www.bbc.com/future/story/20140314-learn-to-be-creative

Baumgartner, J. (2009). *The innovation process.* Retrieved from www.creativejeffrey.com/creative/innovationprocess.php?topic=innovation

Bittman, E. (2014). *How to use creative art projects to make your students love math.* Retrieve from www.weareteachers.com/blogs/post/2014/10/14/9-creative-art-projects-that-will-make-your-students-love-math

Buck Institute for Education. (2015). *Essential project design elements checklist* | Project Based Learning | BIE. Retrieved from http://bie.org/object/document/pbl_essential_elements_checklist

Burrus, D. (2013). *Creativity and innovation: Your keys to a successful organization.* Retrieved from www.huffingtonpost.com/daniel-burrus/creativity-and-innovation_b_4149993.html

Batey, M. (2012). *Creativity is the key skill for the 21st century.* Retrieved from www.creativitypost.com/business/creativity_is_the_key_skill_for_the_21st_century

Batten Institute University of Virginia Darden School of Business. (2015). *How America's education model kills creativity and entrepreneurship.* Retrieved from www.forbes.com/sites/darden/2015/03/19/how-americas-education-model-kills-creativity-and-entrepreneurship-2/#62dce6961ac7

BizKids. (n.d.). *Educational tools.* Retrieved from http://bizkids.com/themes/entrepreneurship

Boss, S. (2013). *Shoe design offers a trojan horse for problem solving with design thinking.* Retrieved from from www.edutopia.org/blog/design-thinking-opportunity-problem-solving-suzie-boss

Bronson, P., & Merryman, S. (2010). *The creativity crisis.* Retrieved from www.newsweek.com/creativity-crisis-74665

Brookhart, S. (2013). Assessing Creativity. *Educational Leadership, 70(5)*, 28–34

Burrus, D. (2013). *Creativity and innovation: Your keys to a successful organization.* Huffington Post Blog. Retrieved from www.huffingtonpost.com/daniel-burrus/creativity-and-innovation_b_4149993.html

College Entrance Examination Board. (2004). *Writing: A ticket to work 000 or a ticket out.* Retrieved from www.collegeboard.com/prod_downloads/writingcom/writing-ticket-to-work.pdf

Church, E. (2012). *How you can help children solve problems.* Retrieved from www.scholastic.com/teachers/article/how-you-can-help-children-solve-problems

Creative Competitions, Inc. (2006). *Odyssey of the mind curriculum activity: Made up math.* Retrieved from https://www.odysseyofthemind.com/materials/made_up_math.php

Davidson, J. (2013). *Gifted students showcase ideas at Invention Convention.* Retrieved from www.gadsdentimes.com/article/DA/20130403/News/603237457/GT/

Davis, R. (2014). *Embracing student creativity with a wonder shelf.* Retrieved May 06, 2016, from www.edutopia.org/blog/embracing-student-creativity-wonder-shelf-rafranz-davis

DeHaan, R. (2011). Teaching creative science thinking. *Science.* 16 Dec 2011 : 1499-150

Ditkoff, M. (2006). *Aha! Great moments in creativity.* Idea Champions, Inc. Retrieved from www.ideachampions.com/article_aha.shtml

E-Line Media & Joan Ganz Cooney Center (2012–2016). *2016 national STEM video game challenge.* Retrieved from http://stemchallenge.org/#/home

Fadel, C. (2015). *Preparing students for the robotic revolution.* Retrieved from www.online-educa.com/OEB_Newsportal/preparing-students-for-the-robotic-revolution/

Florida Department of Education, Bureau of Exceptional Education and Student Services. (2010) *Research-based strategies for problem-solving in mathematics K-12.* Retrieved from http://floridarti.usf.edu/resources/format/pdf/Classroom%20Cognitive%20and%20Metacognitive%20Strategies%20for%20Teachers_Revised_SR_09.08.10.pdf

Fox, Z. (2012). *4 Innovative student projects that could change the world.* Retrieved from http://mashable.com/2012/05/29/microsoft-imagine-cup/

Goodman, S. (2014). *Fuel creativity in the classroom with divergent thinking.* Retrieved from www.edutopia.org/blog/ fueling-creativity-through-divergent-thinking-classroom-stacey-goodman

Gundy, L. (2013). *Boosting creative thinking in math* class | EdWeek.org. Retrieved from http://www.edweek.org/tm/articles/2013/07/09/tln_gundy_math.html

Hiam, Alexander. (2011). *How-and why-to teach innovation in our schools.* eSchoolNews. Retrieved from www.eschoolnews.com/2011/02/01/ how-and-why-to-teach-innovation-in-our-schools/

IBM. (2010). *IBM 2010 global CEO study: Creativity selected as most crucial factor for future success.* Retrieved from www-03.ibm.com/press/us/en/pressrelease/31670.wss

Johnson, D. (2014) Power up! Technology and the illusion of creativity. *Educational Leadership, 71(7)*

Kolk, M. (2012). *5 Hallmarks of a creative project.* Retrieved from http://creativeeducator. tech4learning.com/2012/articles/Creative_Projects

Kuglich, D. (2016). *Persuasive techniques in advertising* | ReadWriteThink. Retrieved from www.readwritethink.org/classroom-resources/lesson-plans/persuasive-techniques-advertising-1166.html

Landergan, K. (2015). BC professor adds hands-on lessons to Chinese schools. *Boston Globe.* 7/12/15

Lapowsky, I. (2014). *Going global? The growing movement to let kids learn just by tinkering.* Retrieved from www.wired.com/2014/10/pencils-of-promise

Long, C. *Six ways the common core is good for students* | NEA Today. Retrieved from http://neatoday.org/2013/05/10/six-ways-the-common-core-is-good-for-students-2/

Millar, E. (2013). *How do Finnish kids excel without rote learning and standardized testing?* | The Globe and Mail. Retrieved from www. theglobeandmail.com/report-on-business/economy/canada-competes/ how-do-finnish-kids-excel-without-rote-learning-and-standardized-testing/article11810188/

National Center for Education Statistics. (2012). *The Nation's Report Card: Writing 2011.* (NCES 2012-470). Institute of Education Sciences, U.S. Department of Education, Washington, D.C.

National Council of Teachers of Mathematics. (2016). *Creative geometry: Introduction*. Retrieved from. http://mathforum.org/sanders/creativegeometry/intro.htm

National Innovation Foundation – India (NIF). (2014). *26 Innovative ideas by school students that will blow your mind away!* Retrieved from www.thebetterindia.com/11596/ignite-innovations/

New York City Department of Education. (n.d.). *Virtual enterprises NYC*. Retrieved from http://schools.nyc.gov/ve/anew/progdescrip.htm

Pennant, J. (2013). *Developing a classroom culture that supports a problem-solving approach to mathematics* | University of Cambridge. Retrieved from http://nrich.maths.org/10341

Pomeroy, S. R. (2012). *From STEM to STEAM: Science and art go hand-in-hand*. Retrieved from http://blogs.scientificamerican.com/guest-blog/from-stem-to-steam-science-and-the-arts-go-hand-in-hand/

Porter, B. (2015). *Six elements of good digital storytelling*. Retrieved from http://creativeeducator.tech4learning.com/v04/articles/Take_Six

Price-Mitchell, M. (2015). *Curiosity: The force within a hungry mind*. Retrieved from www.edutopia.org/blog/8-pathways-curiosity-hungry-mind-marilyn-price-mitchell

Provenzano, N. (2015). *Creativity in the classroom*. Retrieved from www.edutopia.org/blog/creativity-in-the-classroom-nicholas-provenzano

Ragsdale, S. (2013). *Five fun ways to spark self-discovery in youth*. Retrieved May from www.middleweb.com/17540/five-fun-ways-spark-self-discovery-children/

Ramirez, A. (2013). *Creativity is the secret sauce in STEM*. Retrieved from www.edutopia.org/blog/creativity-secret-sauce-in-stem-ainissa-ramirez

Richmond, E. (2012). *The missing link in school reform: Student motivation*. Retrieved from www.theatlantic.com/national/archive/2012/05/the-missing-link-in-school-reform-student-motivation/257770/

Robinson, K. (2014). Can creativity be taught? (video) Uploaded by the Brainwaves Video Anthology

Rodman, J. (2014). *How to design a collaborative environment Steve Jobs would approve of* | Fast Company. Retrieved from www.fastcompany.com/3039404/how-to-design-a-collaborative-environment-steve-jobs-would-approve-of

References

Salcito, A. (2016). *Microsoft invests in new and expanded version of 'Minecraft' for the classroom* | The Official Microsoft Blog. Retrieved from http://blogs.microsoft.com/blog/2016/01/19/

Satell, G. (2014). *How technology enhances creativity.* Retrieved from www.forbes.com/sites/gregsatell/2014/01/27/how-technology-enhances-creativity/#1656c79c483b

Saxena, S. (2013). *How can technology enhance student creativity?* Retrieved from http://edtechreview.in/trends-insights/insights/750-how-can-technology-enhance-student-creativity

Schaffhauser, D. (2012). *Robots rule as competition season heats up* | THE News Update. Retrieved from https://thejournal.com/articles/2012/04/17/robots-rule-as-competition-season-heats-up.aspx?=THENU

Smith, N. (2012). *Who says creativity can't be learned?* | *Business News Daily. Retrieved from* www.businessnewsdaily.com/2471-creativity-innovation-learned.html

Stix, A., & Hrbek, F. (2006). *Teachers as classroom coaches: How to motivate students across the content areas.* Alexandria, VA: Association for Supervision and Curriculum Development.

Teaching Channel. (2016). Persistence in Problem Solving: Grade 3 / Math / Word Problems (video)

Vasicek, B. (2011). *Digital communication: Student-designed commercials* | Scholastic.com. Retrieved from www.scholastic.com/teachers/classroom-solutions/2011/02/digital-communication-student-designed-commercials

White House Office of the Press Secretary. (2009). President Obama launches "Educate to innovate" campaign for excellence in science, technology, engineering & math (press release).

Wiggins, G. (2012). *On assessing for creativity: yes you can, and yes you*

Should. Retrieved from https://grantwiggins.wordpress.com/2012/02/03/on-assessing-for-creativity-yes-you-can-and-yes-you-should/

Zhao, Y. (2014). *Creating the entrepreneurial mindset in 21st century schools* | P21. Retrieved from www.p21.org/news-events/p21blog/1563-creating-the-